TAKING YOUR CAMPUS FOR CHRIST

BARRY ST. CLAIR & KEITH NAYLOR

D1473714

VICTOR BOOKS

A DIVISION OF SCRIPTURE PRESS PUBLICATIONS INC.
USA CANADA ENGLAND

Produced in cooperation with REACH OUT MINISTRIES
3961 Holcomb Bridge Road
Suite 201
Norcross, GA 30092

Cover Design: Paul Higdon
Cartoon Illustrations: Dave and Jesse Lee

ISBN: 1-56476-201-7

2 3 4 5 6 7 8 9 10 Printing/Year 97 96 95 94 93

Acknowledgements

Dave Lee and his 14-year-old son Jesse created the clever cartoons for this book. How exciting to have Jesse and other teenagers have such a heavy influence on this book. I'm not only grateful for the cartoons, but for the relationship. Dave was "Jesus with skin on" to me when I was in high school. He strongly influenced me to give my life to Jesus. For that I am eternally grateful.

Barry St. Clair

Dedication

To the young people in our own families...

Scott		Jena
Katie		Karis
Jonathan		Kase
Ginny		Micah
	St.Clair	Keile
		Tyler
		Cole
		Naylor

...and their generation, who we believe will be the generation to fulfill the Great Commission.

T A K E A L O O K

...AT WHAT'S IN THE BOOK

FOREWORD

"Times are changing with morals in decay,
Human rights have made the wrongs OK
Something's missing, And if your asking me
I think that something is G O D!
We gotta get back to the principles found in the Word
A little G O D could be society's cure
From the state that we're in
'Cause again we're slippin'
So pray for America 'cause time is tickin' "
(from the DC TALK song, "*Socially Acceptable*")

Oh yes, my brothers and sisters! It's gettin' kinda hectic out there. Too much of the "me" and not enough of the "we". Consequently we're moving farther away from the G O D everyday, and strife is taking over. Racism, broken homes, and kids who are finding comfort and truth in a declining moral climate. What's worse is that there are very few alternatives for us. The messages that are sent out via the mass media quench every desire a person probably has except for one: understanding pure, unconditional love, or more precisely, knowing Jesus Christ.

My brother, Barry St.Clair, *is*, however, providing an alternative. He's showing how not only to stay out of the mix of society's craziness, but how to transfer that God-centered love over to your friends. *Taking Your Campus for Christ* is great because it provides people like you and me with an alternative, a way to live in our confusing world and yet not lose our desire to love.

Barry St.Clair is one of those youth ministers who has dared to stay on the edge with both his head and his heart. For 20 years he has made students his life; talked *to* us and not *at* us; for 20 years he has given us an alternative.

In *Taking Your Campus for Christ*, Barry comes straight on, explicit. Facts not fiction is what you'll find in this book 'cause Barry takes us back to the Word. Barry tells us how to bring those around us to the G O D, shows us how he has seen God work time and time again, and gives steps on how to be generous with our knowledge and love for Christ.

Barry St.Clair has got it going on...plain and simple.

"You got a gift and you best start usin' it
'Cause if you don't, you're gonna start losin' it
Just like the brother who buried it deep
The task was simple but the price was steep
We got a mission while we're on this earth
We need to tell people 'bout our second birth
Get busy like a school boy makin' an A
'Cause time, my brother, is tickin' away."
(from the DC TALK song, *Time Is...*)

Toby McKeehan, DC TALK

OUR HOPES AND DREAMS FOR YOU

We had to write this book!

Sensing a mighty movement of God just around the corner, we felt like we had to let you to know our hopes and dreams for your generation.

We believe that God wants to tap you on the shoulder, get you to look Him in the face, and then challenge you with the power of the Gospel—not only for yourself, but also for your friends and your school.

The first Bible verse I learned after I became a Christian was Romans 1:16.
I am not ashamed of the Gospel, because it is the power of God for the salvation of everyone who believes.

This verse is our hope and dream for you. We hope you will experience so much of the power of God in your life that it will cause you not to be ashamed of the Gospel of Christ. We dream that you will boldly proclaim Him to your friends and your school so that many will come to know Jesus Christ.

Our hope and dream is that you will be like Todd.

Entering the sixth grade as a new student in a school with over 1,700 students, he hardly knew anyone. But he did have a desire for people to experience Christ like he had. The first week he came to "See You At The Pole" to pray. Twenty students showed up. So did the principal who told them they could not pray at school. They continued across the street. They wanted to keep meeting. A Christian teacher let them use her classroom. They did this for several weeks until the principal broke up this meeting too. Undaunted, the students met outside around some picnic tables. They were determined to pray for their friends.

And they wanted to reach their friends for Christ too. So they decided to invite their friends to a pancake breakfast. The day arrived. The smell of bacon and pancakes was in the air. But no one came. Discouraged, they all sat down to eat. A few minutes later fifteen "skaters" stormed in. They ate, then listened as these students told about their personal experience with Jesus. The girlfriend of one of Todd's friends accepted Christ. Now they have a pancake breakfast every month.

Because of their desire and determination, by the next year...
- 40 students came to "See You At The Pole".
- A new Christian principal gave them support.
- A campus club had begun with a plan to reach their friends for Christ.
- Todd had led his uncle to Christ. People in the family had talked to his uncle for years, but to no avail. But God used Todd to reach his uncle.
- Three more of Todd's friends came to Christ as a result of Todd sharing Christ with them.

If God can use a little sixth grader to unleash "the power of God," then certainly He can use you!

For the Todds of this world, we have written down what we believe is essential for God to use you to influence your friends and your school for the glory of Jesus Christ. We believe that the total effect of what God will do in you and others like you will result in "the power of the Gospel" bringing your generation to Him.

We hope and dream that God will use you and your generation to fulfill the Great Commission.

Please know that many people are praying for you. And we love you.

Barry and Keith

STEVE'S STORY

Lanier was a school in turmoil. Recently we had undergone mandatory desegregation. Severe racial tension hung in the air. Our public school system was one of three in the nation that separated the boys and girls into different schools. That was because of the problems we were having. The junior high was made up of 8th- and 9th-grade students, with many of the eighth-graders already old enough to drive their own cars.

How was I supposed to fit into the mess at school? I had a big problem. I really wanted to have the same kind of exciting relationship with Jesus as some high school kids I had met during the summer. As much as I wanted to give my life to Jesus, the fear of standing alone at school kept me walking the fence. I had one foot in the youth meetings and one foot in the world. Once, one of my buddies at school said he'd heard I was going to a Bible study. I felt so embarrassed that I swore and told him I was going for the girls.

The turning point came during a Christmas retreat. Out under a tree, between the meetings, I asked the Lord to forgive my sins and take control of my life. I made a solemn commitment to go back to school and raise my flag for Jesus. I wanted to try to win our campus for Christ.

When I returned the next Monday, I immediately experienced Christ's supernatural power in giving me a boldness I'd never had before. Our class had been divided into small "rap" groups that met with the school counselor, Mr. Duck. He was one of those middle-aged men who tried to be cool with the kids. He asked us what we had done over Christmas. I stood up and said, "I accepted Jesus into my life and I want each of you to do it too!"

He responded, "Young man, Christianity is a crutch for the weak." Even though I didn't know how to reply, I stood my ground in the newly discovered power of the Holy Spirit.

I had decided to make a Ten Most Wanted list. I wrote down the names of my ten best friends that I wanted to bring to Christ. Within two months, nine out of ten had accepted Christ. They began to rove the halls with me sharing the Good News of Jesus Christ.

The tenth person on my list was a black student named Roy. Roy was the class clown, and frankly, I held him until last because I wasn't sure how he would react. When I finally did get up the nerve to share with him, he interrupted me halfway through and said, "Now hold it Steve. Don't go too far with this. I've seen it ruin many a man."

Two years later, we were back together in the same homeroom. One day he turned around and saw my Bible. "Is that *The Living Bible?*"

I replied, "Sure, why don't you take it? In fact, why don't you come to our meeting tonight?"

Roy walked two miles in the rain to come to that meeting. At the end, he knelt with me to accept Jesus. The next morning he announced to the class, "You're looking at a new Roy. My main man, Steve, took me to Bible Study last night and I accepted Jesus. "

Looking back on what God did, I found some important elements to taking our campus for Christ.

1.) Our leaders called for us to take the challenge.
They exposed us to joyful, free Christianity. Most Christians I had met looked like they had drunk prune juice before they came to church. But our leaders glowed with a crazy joy that made Christ attractive to us.

But they were not the typical "cookies and kool-aid" types. The requirement to enter a discipleship group was to share the Gospel with at least one person a day, and then report on it. They asked us to memorize a lengthy portion of

Scripture, usually 10–12 verses a week. They taught us the "how to's" of the Christian life. They taught us how to pray, read the Bible, and how to experience the fullness of the Spirit. All of us relished the challenge.

2.) We banded together for prayer. Because the principal was so thrilled at the difference he saw on our campus, he allowed us to have our own conference room to meet in the mornings to pray. We prayed every day before school. We prayed for each other and we prayed for our friends who needed Christ.

3.) We witnessed boldly and aggressively. We shared the good news of Christ with every student in our school! We felt it was our responsibility to see that every student had the chance to receive or reject Christ. We used both creative and reckless tactics in witnessing. For example, I was the sports editor for the school paper. I wrote a full column in every issue on how to know Jesus. During a school dance, we felt such a burden for the lost kids there that during the band's break, we grabbed the microphone, and shared the Gospel. We had four people receive Christ!

I discovered something at Lanier: Once one person raises his flag for Jesus, a whole bunch of others will come out of the closet. We began a junior high Bible study in my living room. Within two months we were averaging over 60 kids. By the end of that year, you could not walk down the hall of our school without seeing about every third student carrying a Bible on top of his books.

If you will take your stand for Christ, and radically love your friends, then Jesus will use you to take your campus for Christ.

(This is the story of Steve Scoggins, from Macon, Georgia.)

CHAPTER 1

Totally Out of Sight

"Image is everything" says *Andre Agassi*

➡ **W**hen you look at the mirror, how do you see yourself?

Describe yourself in 4 words:

1.................................... 3....................................

2.................................... 4....................................

➡ When you walk through the door at school tomorrow, how do you think other people look at you?

Describe how you think they see you in 4 words:

1.................................... 3....................................

2.................................... 4....................................

➡ If you could change two things about the way you see yourself, and two things about the way others see you, what would they be?

Myself

1.................................... 2....................................

Others

1.................................... 2....................................

SOLVE THIS RIDDLE:

What can you see   *that can't be seen*

as already seen *so that it can be seen?*

Oh wow! What does that mean? An architect knows. He pictures in his mind what no one else has seen. After he draws it out on paper, he turns his drawing into reality.

ANSWER TO THE RIDDLE:
Dream/Imagination.

> God wants to do more in and through you on your campus than you can see or imagine now!

➡ Stretching your imagination to the max, what is the greatest thing you can possibly imagine God doing through you on your campus?
Describe that in one sentence.

••

••

Check out what He did through one student:

Because of my parents' divorce, I rebelled and chunked it all. Raised in the black ghetto, I got into drugs when I was nine. When I moved to an Hispanic ghetto, I got into a gang called, "The Devil's Children." In my school 60% of the kids were black, 39% were Hispanic, and 1% were white. The blacks would chant: "We want black power." The Hispanics: "We want Chicano power." The whites: "We want out of here."

Then the pastor of a small church drove by the school one day. He prayed, "Lord, would You give me that school?" The Lord responded: "I've given it to you. Go tell the principal."

What God didn't tell him was that the principal was an atheist. The principal said to him: "Kids are getting busted, smoking marijuiana, carrying guns. . . . What can you do for this school?"

The pastor said, "Nothing. But Jesus can."

Finally the principal relented. "I'll give you 30 minutes for an assembly."

The pastor replied: "The Lord told me I could have an hour."

In the assembly I jumped up and mocked: "Here I am, Jesus. Save me. Change me." The pastor invited everyone to a meeting that night. At 5 'o clock Delores, the pretty girl next door, invited me to go. I said, "I've had enough of that religious garbage." She smiled this really pretty smile, so I said I'd go. I sat with my friends. We set off firecrackers. And we did everything else we could to disrupt. At the end 100 people went forward to accept Christ. I wanted out of there.

The black guy who was talking to Delores began to talk to me. I thought he would say: "You wicked little Mexican punk...robbing, raping, and stealing...." Instead, he said, "Jacob, no matter what you've done, Jesus Christ can forgive you and change your life."

That night I said, "God if You are real, change me."

Right there the Lord brought a scene to my mind: I saw my dad dragging me to a bar when I was nine. After beating up the man who was with my mom, he said, "Look at your mom. She's a whore." In that moment, when I received Jesus, all the hatred disappeared that I had for both of my parents.

I knew Jesus had changed me when I went to Mr. Cheesman. In the seventh grade I had stood right in front of him and gave him the finger. Now I was asking him to forgive me.

During the next week 1,000 students gave their lives to Jesus at our school. A room was designated where teachers could send students who were interested in knowing Christ. All day long the room was filled.

One thousand kids met every morning before school.

15

One morning we took up the drugs that kids were no longer using. The pastor took a trash bag full to the principal. He kept saying, "I can't believe it." And he gave his life to Christ right there. Our entire school changed.[1]

Just as He changed Jacob's life and school, the Lord has made a promise to you that He will do the same through you!

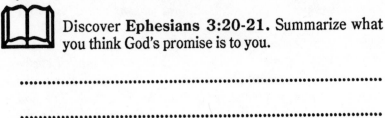 Discover **Ephesians 3:20-21.** Summarize what you think God's promise is to you.

....

....

Already God is working!

> God wants
> to use you beyond your
> wildest imagination
> to change your generation!

▷ Around the world:

Seventy percent of all of the progress in evangelizing the world has happened since 1900; 70% of that has happened since World War II. And 70% of that has happened in the last three years!

What a fantastic time in history to be alive!

▷ On the campus:

Two million young people gathered to pray at "See You At The Pole." That was the largest prayer meeting in history! Six thousand students have come to Christ on the campuses in Wichita, Kansas in one year.

▷ Through people like you:

Take my friend, Brandon, whose school refused to allow "See You At The Pole." Brandon went to the flagpole, stood alone, and prayed. The next year the school allowed "See You At The Pole" and about 75 students gathered to pray because of Brandon's influence.

TAKE THE CHALLENGE

You may be thinking...

- "I'm not going to yell, 'Jesus saves' over the school intercom."
- "I've never even prayed out loud before."
- "I'm not up for this. I hate challenges."
- "Besides nobody I know gives a rip about God."

This isn't about charging the gates of hell with a squirt gun. But it is about what God wants to do in and through you with your friends on your campus.

➡ What is it going to take for you to make a radical difference on your campus?

From **John 1:35-42** write down what you think John is saying to you about that.

....

....

When Jesus talked to John and Andrew, He asked them this incredibly simple question: "What do you want?"

Jesus cuts through all of the baloney and gets down to the real meat of the matter. He goes straight to their motives.

WHAT DO YOU WANT?

➡ Isn't that a great question? Why don't you answer it for yourself? I mean, if you could have anything, do anything, be anyone:

John and Andrew could see 👁 one answer from God's point of view. God wants you to see 👁 from the same point of view so you can make a difference on your campus

COME WITH JESUS

➡ John and Andrew wanted to come with Jesus, so they asked Him, "Where are You staying?" And what does He tell them? (v. 39)

Where is He going? They don't have a clue! But they are so fascinated with Him that they will follow Him anywhere.

"THE SACRIFICE PART I DON'T MIND, AS LONG AS I DON'T HAVE TO GIVE UP MY STEREO, CAR, SPORTS, TV, OR TIME!"

Discover how Jesus described it in **Matthew 16:24**.

●●●

> To "deny" means we have to make choices.

▷ CHOICES ABOUT "STUFF"

To come with Jesus, you give it all to Him. What specific, practical decisions do you need to make about your stuff?

—How you spend your money?

●●●

—The way you spend your time?

●●●

—What you do with your possessions?

●●●

▷ CHOICES ABOUT WHAT OTHER PEOPLE HAVE DONE TO YOU.

To come with Jesus means that you toss your old baggage that other people have given to you to carry. Check below the baggage you need to drop off?

      ❑ your parents' divorce
      ❑ breaking up with your boyfriend/girlfriend
      ❑ a friend who has turned his/her back on you
      ❑ abusive parents
      ❑ other...

▷ CHOICES YOU HAVE MADE.

To come to Jesus, we turn our backs on our old attitudes

and actions. Decide which of these you need to turn your back on.

☐ drinking   ☐ sex
☐ drugs   ☐ cheating
☐ bad language   ☐ disrespect for parents
☐ other...

Every morning my daughter, Katie, leaves for school with a very heavy backpack, a duffle bag, a couple of changes of clothes, a pocketbook, and other stuff. She walks to the car doubled over from the weight. The physically loaded-down feeling that Katie has may be the way you feel spiritually. From some of the choices you have made, or others have made for you, you feel weighted down.

GOOD NEWS!

Jesus made you a promise in **Matthew 11:28-29.** What does this promise mean to you?

....

....

➠ You can unload it all when you come with Jesus! Ask Jesus to take the load you are carrying now.

Jesus, I give the baggage of these choices, to you:

1...

2...

3...

I release these to You. I don't want to carry these anymore.

SPEND TIME WITH JESUS

John and Andrew took Jesus up on His invitation. John 1:39 says, "So they went...and spent the day with Him." They dropped what they were doing. They weren't too busy. They gave Him their undivided attention.

How much of your undivided attention does Jesus get? Let's take a quiz and find out. Mark your answers below.

How many hours a week do you spend:
✶ playing Nintendo____   ✶ having a Quiet Time____
✶ watching TV____   ✶ attending youth group___
✶ talking on the phone____ ✶ talking to God____

How many can you quote word for word:
☐ song lyrics from the radio____
☐ Bible verses____

How much money do you spend each month on:
○ clothes____
○ tithe and other money spent on "God's stuff"____

Total up the numbers in each column and see for yourself.
△ amount of time and money on "my stuff"_____
△ amount of time and money on "God's stuff"_____

Pretty revealing, huh? But if you are going to take the challenge to make a difference on your campus, then it sure helps to get an honest grasp on what grabs your attention.

➡ Now, let's think about how you can begin to shift your resources from "your stuff" to "God's stuff." Any ideas? Right now ask God what He would like you to do. Write down what He shows you.

••

••

Two thoughts in case you weren't sure what to write:

21

1.) Begin a 15- to 30-minute time with God every day.

2.) Start to meet with one or two friends at school to pray. (Later on we will show you how to do these so you will be successful at them.)

Doing these two things will mean you are spending more time with God everyday.

> "The greatest thing anyone can do for God and for man is to pray. It is not the only thing. But it is the chief thing. The great people of the earth today are the people who pray. I do not mean those who talk about prayer; nor those who say they believe in prayer; nor yet those who can explain about prayer; but I mean those people who take time to pray. IF THEY HAVE NOT TIME... IT MUST BE TAKEN FROM SOMETHING ELSE." (S.D. Gordon)

➡ Will you take the challenge to give your undivided attention to the Lord?

Lord Jesus, I give my undivided attention to You.
I want to change the way I use my time by:

....
I want to change the way I use my possessions by:

....
I want to change the way I use my money by:

....

I want my attention to focus 👁 on You and Your purposes for me and my friends at school.

BRING PEOPLE TO JESUS

After Andrew and John came to Jesus and after they had spent time with Him, they wanted all of their relatives and friends to know Him. So what was "the first thing" Andrew did? (verse 41)

....

....

➡ Most young Christians, unlike Andrew and John, get uptight about "letting their light shine" outside the church. What are your top three fears about telling your friends at school about Jesus? Why do you feel that way?

FEAR	FEELING
(1)	....
(2)	....
(3)	....

To begin to turn your fear to faith examine these Bible verses.

What does Jesus tell you the mission is in **Matthew 28:19?**

....

What two gifts does Jesus give us to take on the mission? (See verses 18 and 20.)

(1) ....

(2) ....

Why did He give you those two gifts? To take the pressure off!! Now you don't have to rely on your own ability, your own words, your own faith. You have His authority, His presence! What else do you need? Nothing! Now you can relax about "taking your campus." It's not your job. It's His job. He just wants to use your body to get the job done.

That means you don't have to be nervous about what you will say to people, or focus on yourself and how you are coming across. Instead, you can focus on the presence of Jesus who lives in you, and let His power work to change your friends and your school.

My son, Scott, goes to the university. He is the only Christian in his fraternity, although he meets with a group of Christians weekly. He has taken a stand for Jesus Christ without condemning his friends. Once some guys in his fraternity asked Scott what he was going to do with his future. He said, "I want to be a medical missionary." They said, "Oh, you're getting your brownie points with God." Scott's reply: "I don't need any brownie points with God. I've got all I need. But He has changed my life and I would like to tell you about it sometime." They invited him to their room and they talked about Jesus for over an hour!

God wants to use you like that on your campus. If you are willing to take the challenge, then we will show to how to make a difference.

* * * * *

I take the challenge to take my campus for Christ.

*Signed*_____

NOW GET READY TO HELP HURTING FRIENDS

1. Jacob Aranza's story is quoted from the videotape, "Turning Your Campus Right Side Up."
2. George Otis Jr. National and International Religion Report, 1993

CHAPTER 2

Completely Lacking

> "I'm paranoid. I do this and I do that.
> I can buy anything I want. I can have anything I want,
> but I'm still not happy.
> I wonder why I'm not happy?"
>
> *Eddie Murphy*

Tomorrow you will stand on a cafeteria table and announce that you have the answer to everyones' problems. Anyone who wants to talk about how Jesus can give them life will be welcome to talk to you after lunch. If you did that, what do you think would happen?

- People would beg for forgiveness including the teacher who put you in detention yesterday.
- You would get hit in the eye with a chicken fajita.
- A heath class representative would hand you a condom.
- People would call you a "weirdo Jesus freak" and label you a danger to society.
- People would stay and listen respectfully.

What percentage of the students at your school do you think are interested in hearing about God?

Circle the percentage you estimate is correct.

0% 10% 20% 30% 40% 50% 60% 70% 80% 90% 100%

➡ What do you think is the major reason people at your school are not interested in hearing about God's love for them?

One major reason followers of Christ don't talk about Jesus with others is that they don't believe people want to know about God. But the truth is often people build walls around their lives, so *it seems* that they have no interest in knowing about God.

All week Jimmie had gone through her school activities totally detached emotionally. Beautiful and athletic, but plainly withdrawn, it was as if she wore a sign around her neck: "Stay Away." But one day she began to open up. Then it became clear why she had such a hard exterior.

One year ago that day she had overheard her father answer her mother's question, "What about the kids?" As the mother begged with him not to leave her, he said, "I don't give a @#$%^ about those kids!"

That was the last time Jimmie had seen her father in her home.

EVERY 24 HOURS
in the lives of U.S.A.'s young people
2,989 children see their parents get divorced.
2,556 children are born out of wedlock.
1,629 children are in adult jails.
3,288 children run away from home.
1,849 children are abused or neglected.
1,512 teenagers drop out of school.
437 children are arrested for drinking or drunken driving.
211 children are arrested for drug abuse.
2,795 teens (women under 20) get pregnant.
7,742 teenagers become sexually active.
1,106 teenagers have abortions.
1,295 teenagers give birth.
372 teenagers miscarry.
623 teenagers contract syphilis or gonorrhea.
6 teenagers commit suicide [1]

She told me that day, "I decided at that time I would never let my heart trust again so it would never be hurt again."

As she talked tears formed in her eyes, then flowed down her face, then turned into an uncontrollable sob. All the hurt she had held in for a year came flooding out.

Many people at your school are like Jimmie. They have a hard exterior, but deep inside they are hurting.

That was true of a man names Zacchaeus too. We will call him"Zack the Lack" because he was lacking love

 Read **Luke 19:1-8.**

➡ What clues do you find that show Zacchaeus had a hard exterior?

••

••

➡ What other clues do you find that Zack was hurting?

••

••

"Zack the Lack" was one of the last people on Planet Earth you would have picked to show an interest in God. As a tax collector, everyone hated him because he ripped off people's money. And they couldn't do anything about it. Tax collectors were lower than a worm's belly!

Zack was a chief tax collector, which meant he took a percentage from what all the other tax collectors collected. Add in the fact that he was short, and Zack had a serious case of low self-esteem. But he projected an image that he had no need for others and didn't really care what they thought. Yet deep inside Zack was hurting because of this rejection.

People don't want to get hurt more. Have you ever had a bruise or cut that hurt so badly that any time someone got close to you, you got tense? To protect themselves from the hurt, people act like they do not care. They form a hard exterior to keep people away.

Jimmie's poem explains this powerfully.

> As I sit looking into the mirror
> The reflection I see,
> Is that of a girl
> with the appearance of being carefree.
>
> The mirror reflections do not show
> The things going on inside
> Those feelings buried deep inside
> Would make any other run and hide
>
> These feelings are kept so hidden
> and because they are so well protected
> to anyone on the outside
> They are impossible to be detected
>
> Finding no one to talk to
> No one who seems to care
> Without someone to lean on
> These feelings I myself must bear
>
> To whoever said this

That mirrors do not lie
You are gravely mistaken
for the truth I know inside!

➧ Think of one experience where you were rejected or hurt. What happened? How did you feel?

....

....

....

➧ Right now, ask Jesus to handle your hurt and rejection. Write it in a prayer.

....

....

....

SALLY, I'VE GOT SOMETHING TO SAY, BUT I DON'T WANT TO **HURT** YOU.

1.

HURT ME? OH, JOEY, LIFE IS FULL OF HURTS. MY PARENTS SPLIT UP... I WRECKED MY CAR. I'VE LEARNED TO BE TOUGH. HURTS DON'T **HURT** NOW.

2.

I THINK WE SHOULD START DATING OTHER PEOPLE.

3.

4.

Under every tough veneer lies a heart that was created in the image of God and yearning to know God. Let's dispel the myth that a person's bad reputation, weird behavior, hard exterior or arrogance means that he or she is not interested in knowing God.

2. EVERY 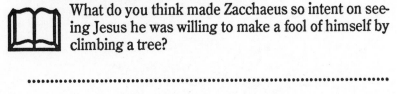 LONGS FOR LOVE.

The reason Zack lacked is that he looked for love in all the wrong places.

- PEOPLE
    - PROSPERITY
        - PARTIES
            - POSITION

But none of it satisfied him. His theme song might be, "I can't get no satisfaction."

But today would be different. The Bible says, "He wanted to see who Jesus was," (Luke 19:3).

We often write people off because they do not appear interested in the things of God. In reality they desperately hope for and search for proof that love really exists in a world that has hurt them so much.

What do you think made Zacchaeus so intent on seeing Jesus he was willing to make a fool of himself by climbing a tree?

••

••

Word was out that Jesus was coming that way He had forgiven the sins of a prostitute. Could it be true? Could Jesus really love no matter what?

Like Zacchaeus, Jimmie hoped for love, but wondered if she would ever find it.

I feel as if I'm sinking
Into a never-ending ditch
The walls are caving in around me
God, life is such a bitch!

Could there be another out there
Who feels the same way as I?
How do they survive
In this world where I want to die?

I wish I had someone
I could tell my secrets to
without them running off
and telling everyone they knew.

➡ Name one person at your school who is desperately searching for love:

....

➡ What kinds of attitudes and actions do they exhibit that shows they are looking for love?

1. ....

2. ....

3. ....

➡ Think of one specific way you could show love to that person?

....

....

3. EVERY 💚 CAN BE MADE WHOLE BY JESUS.

When Jesus called Zack to come down out of the tree, he experienced Jesus' love for the first time. "Zack the Lack" was lacking no more!

Zack changed from living on empty to living on full all in one experience with Jesus. In fact, he had so much of the love of Jesus flowing out of him, he had to share it. He became a giver.

➡ What did Zack do once he saw that Jesus actually wanted to spend time with him?

"So he came down at once and welcomed him gladly...Zacchaeus stood up and said, "Look Lord! Here and now I give half of my possessions to the poor, and if I have cheated anybody out of anything, I will pay back four times the amount."

••

••

When Zacchaeus met Jesus, he was never the same again. The same will be true for your friends when they meet Jesus through you!

> "There is a God-shaped vacuum in the heart of every man that cannot be filled by any created thing, but only by God the creator made known through Jesus Christ."
>
> *Pensées,* Pascal
> World-renowned scientist

Jesus is calling Jimmie down out of the tree too. But like some of your friends, she is not quite there yet. In her words:

I'm still looking to see if God's love is real in the world I live in. It is still too big a jump to take. I just can not take being hurt again.

But Bryan has come all the way to Jesus.

Bryan had begun to show interest in knowing more about Jesus Christ, but when his father died suddenly of a heart attack, he turned totally away. In a conversation he said, "Anyone who would take my father from me, I don't want to know about." After several pleas with Bryan to take a closer look at Jesus Christ, it was plain to see that he wasn't interested. He continued his life of partying and running around with girls and avoided anyone who had anything to do with Jesus Christ. His Christian friends never gave up and continued to reach out to him and love him no matter Bryan's response to them. After five years of loving Bryan, one of his Christian friends got a call from Bryan late one night. He was crying and needed someone who cared about and loved him. That night Bryan gave his life to Christ, and in a letter to his friend said:

"Thank you for being there for me throughout the worst of times. Thank you for loving me and not giving up when I didn't care...Love in Christ, Bryan."

Many of your friends are like Zacchaeus, Jimmie, and Bryan. Even though they may cover it up really well, they have empty, broken hearts. They long for love. And they can only find it in a personal relationship with Jesus. Through you, Jesus is passing by every day...by their lockers, by their classrooms, passing them in the halls, and in the cafeteria. Through you, Jesus wants to call them to "come down" and meet Him.

➡ Ask God to break your heart for the broken hearts of your friends. Write down your prayer to Him.

••

••

★ ★ ★ ★ ★

I want God to use me to reach my hurting friends.

*Signed*_____

NOW GET READY TO AWESOMELY EXPERIENCE GOD!

¹Children's Defense Fund. 1/8/90

CHAPTER 3

Awesomely Experiencing God

"Far better is it to dare mighty things,
to win glorious triumphs even
though checkered by failure,
than to rank with those
poor spirits who neither enjoy
nor suffer much because
they live in the gray twilight
that knows neither victory
nor defeat."

Teddy Roosevelt[1]

When you lie in your bed on one of those nights when you are thinking about life, how do you know for sure that God is real? Circle one or more of the following:

⇨You saw a shooting star on your birthday.

⇨Your mom and dad said so.

⇨Your big brother went off to college and you got his room.

⇨You asked someone out on a date and that person said yes.

⇨Your algebra teacher was sick on exam day and passed everyone.

⇨Your dad didn't notice when you didn't fill the car back up with gas.

⇨You didn't have to kiss great Aunt Mary's hairy lips at the family reunion.

⇨You experience God's power and presence in your life every day.

In answer to Oprah Winfrey's question on why he does so much for terminally ill children, Michael Jackson said, "I try to imitate Jesus." Later he was asked, "Do you have anything in your life that is for sure?" To this he responded with confidence: "No."

I'm not sure where Michael Jackson is in his relationship with God, but one thing is sure: He isn't that different from the majority of people who call themselves Christians. They speak highly of Jesus. They may even pattern part of their lives after Jesus, but deep down they are not really sure that Jesus is real. They have not experienced the presence and power of God in their lives.

If you are going to tell others about Christ effectively then you must talk about Him from your own personal experience.

Personal experience makes all the difference. For example, the way you tell someone about the new roller coaster you heard advertised on TV at Six Flags is one thing. The way you tell about the new roller coaster that you personally rode 20 times until you threw up on your best friend is another!

You need to know without a doubt that you are experiencing God's presence and power in your life daily.

➡ Recall two times that you felt close to God. What was happening? Where were you? What were the circumstances that made God seem so real?

1..

....

2..

....

Possibly you have felt so close to God that it was as if He was with you physically. Or maybe you have never felt particularly close to God.

Either way, God wants you to experience Him every day! The Apostle Peter spent more time with Jesus physically than any other person. From his encounter with Jesus in **Matthew 14:25-31,** what do you discover about how to experience God's presence and His power?

....

....

....

BELIEVE JESUS FOR THE IMPOSSIBLE!
Of all the disciples, Peter was the only one who actually believed that it was Jesus walking on the water. That's understandable. It isn't every day that you see some guy walking across the lake without a Ski Nautique.

➡ After seeing Jesus perform miracle after miracle, why do you think the disciples still doubted that He could walk on water?

....

....

➡ Today, after 2,000 years of Jesus accomplishing the impossible again and again, people still respond the way the disciples did. Give three reasons why you think people (possibly including you) doubt that Jesus can do the impossible.

1..

2..

3..

39

If we experience the presence of an all powerful God every day, then we wouldn't struggle so much to believe Him for the impossible.

Jim Elliot, the famous missionary murdered by the cannibals he tried to reach with the love of Jesus, said, "I have prayed for new miracles. Explaining old miracles will not do. If God is to be known as the god who does wonders in heaven and earth, then God must produce for this generation."

After Jim Elliot was shot to death with arrows by the Auca Indians his wife, Elisabeth, went back with their daughter to live among the Auca's to share the love of Christ. In time, hundreds of people in that tribe accepted Christ—including one of the men who killed her husband. Today the majority of the Aucas are followers of Christ. The man who killed Jim Elliot is the pastor of one of the churches.[3]

For God to become real to you, you must believe that He is present and powerful, and that He can do anything.

➡ What kind of miracle do you want to believe God for in your life, family, or campus? (Be specific.)

....

....

LEAVE EVERYTHING ELSE TO COME TO JESUS.
It's one thing to believe something in your mind. It's another to put it into action with your body.

Of all the disciples, it appears that Peter was the only one who took a single step toward getting out of the boat.

➡ If you had been in Peter's sandals, why would you have either stayed in the boat or gotten out?

Stayed In:..

Gotten Out: ....

➡ If you had been the one swinging your leg over the side of the boat, what would have been going through your mind? ....

....

One reason people don't experience God is that they don't have anything to trust Him for. Or if they do have something, they refuse to step over the side and let go.

For example, Krissy accepted Christ, but still carried

on a physical relationship with her boyfriend. Her friend challenged her to give Christ all of her life, including her sexual relationship with her boyfriend. Krissy responded, "I will give Christ anything but that, that is the only thing I can't give up."

She was unwilling to step out of the boat and trust Christ with her boyfriend. Krissy stayed in the "comfort zone" of the boat, afraid that if she let go, Jesus would let her down.

But I believe most students want to have the courage to step out like this young man:

Under Communist rule, Christians in Romania suffered persecution from the government. The police picked up a teenage boy from a Christian family for questioning. This common practice was designed to separate the young people from their parents' faith. The large officer took off his belt and popped it as he questioned the boy. Then the officer told him to make a choice. "Choose to play soccer and go to school, or choose to believe in a God who doesn't exist." The boy pondered for a moment, then stood up. With tears in his eyes he said, "You can take my soccer and you can take my education, but you can never, ever take away my faith in my Lord Jesus Christ."

That's taking the big leap!

➡ Which of the two people just described experienced more of the power and presence of God?

••

➡ Where do you struggle with stepping out of the boat?

❑ Athletic success
❑ Relationship to your boyfriend or girlfriend
❑ Communicating with your parents
❑ Bitterness toward someone who has hurt you
❑ Money

❏ Popularity/reputation
❏ Sexual desires
❏ Studying /grades
❏ Car
❏ The future
❏ Witnessing to your friends
❏ Something else not mentioned here _____

➠ What one thing in your life do you most enjoy doing?

....

....

➠ If that were taken away from you, do you believe that Christ could actually fill the void?

Yes ❏   No ❏

Jumping out of the boat into the seemingly uncertain future can be frightening.

Vicki expresses it this way as I challenged her to take a step of faith: "It's like jumping off a cliff and not knowing whether someone will catch you or not."

Sure it's frightening, but there is more to the story!

STEP OUT TO EXPERIENCE JESUS' POWER AND PRESENCE.
It didn't work. Peter sank! Yeah, he stepped out—but he sank. He wiped out. He blew it. He didn't have enough faith. He saw a couple of Barracuda licking their chops, and BAM, he's drinking the ultimate uncola.

➠ But wait! Is that it? Nope. The "Peter Blows It Again" saga continues. Read the story again and see if you can find what happened that positively changed the rest of Peter's life.

1. ....

2. ....

PETER EXPERIENCED THE POWER OF GOD.

Check it out! Peter actually walked on the water! None of the other disciples did that. When was the last time you did it? It's not something you just go out and do every day. You see bungee jumpers, sky divers, cliff climbers, but no water walkers. The only way Peter pulled that off was by God's power.

What do you think this did for Peter's faith? Imagine Peter's interview with Dick Vitale on ESPN. After video footage and Peter's comments, Dick Vitale says: "He walked on water. We're talking H_2O, baby! Human hydroplane! He walked where Flipper flipped!"

Peter's life would never be the same because he actually experienced the power of God. Once you experience His power you will never be the same either.

➡ Practically, what one step do you need to take toward Jesus to experience His power?

....

....

PETER EXPERIENCED THE PRESENCE OF GOD.

News Update: "Today the Apostle Peter drowned while trying to walk across the lake. Allegedly Jesus was on the water too, but refused to do anything to help."

NOT! So if that's not the story, what is?

Before Peter even got his Speedo wet, Jesus reached out His hand. Right there, Peter touched the presence of God. Because none of the other disciples took the risk, none of them got to experience Jesus' strong hand.

I was playing basketball for the number-three team in the nation. My future looked bright. But I knew that as a new Christian, basketball overshadowed my walk with Christ. One day I had the thought: "Maybe you shouldn't be playing basketball." I dismissed it as a ridiculous thought, because I had played basketball all my life. I had prepared for years for this time, sweeping the snow off the court in the winter, and practicing eight hours a day in

44

the summer.

A little later I read Matthew 6:33, "Seek first God's kingdom and His righteousness." I knew basketball was more important to me than my relationship with God. In the hardest decision I've ever made, I stepped out of the boat and gave up my basketball scholarship. I thought I would have a huge void in my life.

But to show you how neat God is, within a week I got involved in working with young people—now my life's work. If I had not quit basketball, I would never have met the people who got me involved in working with young people. And, check this out, within a year the Lord put me on a national and international team that played college and university teams all over the United States and around the world. At halftime and after the game we would present the good news of Christ to thousands of people. Now instead of playing for myself, I played for Him!

When we step out of the boat, Jesus always comes through!

➡ What areas of your life do you want to "walk on water" and see the power and presence of God at work?

- ☐ Anger
- ☐ Your weight
- ☐ Your parents' relationship
- ☐ Discipline
- ☐ Your youth group
- ☐ Christians unified at school
- ☐ Friends coming to Christ
- ☐ Fear
- ☐ Sexual thoughts
- ☐ Broken relationships
- ☐ Worry
- ☐ Your best friend stealing your girlfriend
- ☐ Low self-esteem
- ☐ The "want" monster
- ☐ Standing up to temptation/pressure
- ☐ Grades
- ☐ Athletics
- ☐ Other

➡ Pick the one where you most want to see God demonstrate His power.

•••

➡ Express to God in your own words that you are "letting go and letting God" release His power and presence to meet your need.

•••

•••

•••

TAKE THE PLUNGE!
Sure it's scary. You're right, you lose control. Definitely, it's a big risk. But how will you ever know if Jesus really "works" unless you put your leg over the side of the boat, let go, and take a faith walk? It's a big step toward God using you on your campus. Go for it! Jesus has you by the hand!

* * * * *

I have decided to take the risk to be used powerfully by God.

Signed_____

NOW GET READY FOR GOD TO CHANGE
YOUR CHARACTER

[1] Charles R. Swindoll, Come Before Winter (Portland, Ore., Multnomah Press, 1985) p. 197.

[2] Chuck Colson, The Body (Dallas, Word Publishing, 1992), p. 186.

[3] (From *The Journals of Jim Elliot,* Edited by Elisabeth Elliot (Old Tappen, N.J., Fleming H. Revell, 1978), pp. 173-74.

Chapter 4
Definitely Changing and Rearranging

Character: Who you are
when nobody else is around.

What if, when the principal makes announcements tomorrow, he instructs all of the students in the school to turn in written reports of everything they have ever seen you do. What would the people at your school write?

- "He is real obnoxious when he drinks."
- "When he took me out, I thought he was a nice guy, but he turned out to be a sex maniac"
- "I've seen her cheat on several tests."
- "His mouth is straight from the garbage can."
- "She talks about her friends behind their backs."

➡ What do you think they would write about you?

••

••

BIG PROBLEM: Your friends know about the negative things you have done in the past or that you are still doing now. As a Christian, you've blown it! You want to change your image, and even more importantly, your lifestyle. You know this is absolutely essential if you are going to make a difference on your campus. What do you do?

FOCUS ON CHARACTER! Without CHARACTER (what's on the inside of us,) we destroy our LIFESTYLE and RELATIONSHIPS (what appears on the outside).

Let's say your dad buys you a brand new Porsche. (Dream on!) The first few days you drive it you are really careful. "Nobody better even get a fingerprint on my car." But then you get used to driving it. You begin to wheel and squeal through the traffic. You take the speed bumps at school at 65 mph. Then one Saturday your friends want to go for a drive in the country. Out of the city you fly along the two-lane roads. Your friends talk you into taking the car off the highway down a very dusty road. Dust is flying everywhere. Eventually they talk you into driving off the road and through the fields. You brush a few trees and scrape some paint off. Then BAM! You hit a big rock. Now you are asking yourself: "What am I doing? How did I let them talk me into this? Why am I treating my beautiful, expensive car like this?"

Possibly you have treated your life like that car was treated. God has given you a Porsche, but you haven't taken care of it.

"Since most of us would rather be admired for what we *do*, rather than for what we *are*, we are normally willing to sacrifice character for conduct, and integrity for achievement." (Sydney J. Harris, columnist, *Chicago Sun-Times*)

We get on a dusty, bumpy road that destroys character by thinking that right and wrong are determined by what helps me.

Right is what helps me achieve happiness.

Wrong is what keeps me from achieving happiness.

We think the most important thing in life is to be happy. You say: "Doesn't God want me to be happy"? Actually He is more interested in your being HOLY! He is interested in your character. When that is growing, you will be happy.

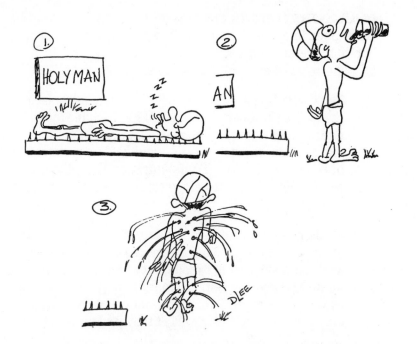

We stay on the freeway of character as we learn to follow Jesus. He keeps our Porsche cleaned and filled.

Developing character means you are learning how to

1) Come to the cross to get **cleaned up** from your sin. (All the stuff the principal would have said over the intercom.)

2) Call on the Holy Spirit to get **filled up** with the character of Jesus Christ.

"How does that work?" you ask. (I'm glad you did!)

Simon Peter, who seemed to always struggle with himself, shows us how.

- Peter was the disciple who had "foot in mouth" disease. Every time he opened his mouth he stuck his foot in it. (Here's a question: If Peter had both feet in his mouth, did he have to walk on his hands?) At the high and holy moment of the Transfiguration, he yells out at Jesus, "Hey, Jesus, this is great. Can we stay up here and camp out?"

- Brash is a word that fit Peter well. When Jesus told His men He was going to die on the cross, Peter pulls Him aside and tells Him, "Jesus, let's get this straight. I know You are the Son of God and all, but there's no way You are going to die. You can count on it because old Peter said so." Jesus wasn't real fired up about that.

- Lack of self-control haunted Peter. In the Garden of Gethsemane Jesus asked him to watch and pray. Instead, he cut Zs with the rest of the disciples. That happened three times. Then when he woke up, he took out his sword and cut a guy's ear off.

- But Peter's worst nightmare became reality. He told Jesus that he would never deny Him, but would follow Him to death. Then Peter denied Jesus three times. After that one, he cried.

Peter smashed his car into a big tree!

➡ How was Peter, who denied Jesus and was restored, different from Judas, who betrayed Jesus and committed suicide?

....

....

PETER REPENTED!

Judas only felt sorry for what he did, but Peter repented and did something about it.

Repent means to
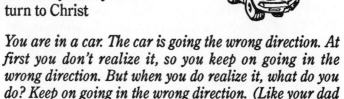
- turn away from your sin
- turn to Christ

You are in a car. The car is going the wrong direction. At first you don't realize it, so you keep on going in the wrong direction. But when you do realize it, what do you do? Keep on going in the wrong direction. (Like your dad does!) No way! That's stupid. You turn around. You turn away from the wrong direction and you turn in the right direction.

That's what repentance is pure and simple.

Simply feeling sorry about going the wrong way won't help. *You must turn around!*

It's more than something you do once just before you receive Christ. ("Repent and be saved.") Rather it is a moment by moment attitude. So, whether or not you repent depends on your attitude right now. You can be in the junkyard of sin, miserable big time, and still not repent. Or you can humble yourself before God right now, and submit to His cleaning up process in your life.

Something else: real repentance, the kind that produces character, does not come through your disciplined efforts to do better. If you could have done better you would have done so already. No, it is the recognition that we have to die to our own efforts and let God help us.

This is so hard for us. We only want to deal with external changes. But Jesus wants a deep change in the attitudes of our hearts.

LIES WE BELIEVE

What got us in this mess? We lie to ourselves.

- "That's just the way I am."
  (God, who had the power to create the whole universe, You can't change me.)
- "But I wasn't the only one."

(Since everybody else does it, certainly God doesn't take it seriously.)

- "I don't see any harm in it."
  (Since I'm the final judge, if I don't think anything is wrong with it, then there must not be anything wrong.)
- "I'll just try it once."
  (If I do it once, there won't be any consequences.)
- "Who's going to know?"
  (As long as nobody knows, it's OK.)
- "But I love him/her"
  (My happiness is more important than obedience.)
- "I don't listen to the words."
  (What I hear repeatedly will not influence me.) [1]

All of us are tempted by these kinds of lies all the time. And we have believed them.

For years I believed a lie. I had cheated in college on some tests. I knew it was wrong. When I thought about it, I felt guilty. But I thought, "Nobody knows but God and me." So for years I thought about it, felt guilty, but never honestly dealt with it. I was afraid to deal with it, because I knew I would have to go back to the professor and confess. I didn't want other people to know. I thought I might lose my degree. Finally when I realized that God would not leave me alone, I confessed it. I told God about it (as if He didn't already know). The scariest part was calling the professor. I'll never forget the day I shut the door, picked up the phone, and called him. I was so frightened, I wanted to hang up. With a trembling voice I said, "Dr._____ when I was in your class I cheated on some tests. I'm a follower of Christ, and I realize that was wrong. Will your forgive me?" When he said "yes," I almost floated out of the room. I was free!

➤ What would you say is the one glaring lie that you have believed?

••

What recurring sin do you need to repent of?

What does **1 John 1:9** promise will happen when we confess our sin?

●●

●●

➡ What step of action do you need to take to make your repentance complete?

●●

●●

"Change, as our Lord describes it, involves more than cleaning up our visible act. He intends us to do more than sweep the streets: He wants us to climb down into the sewer and do something about the filth." (*Inside Out*, Larry Crabb, p. 32)

55

To live life as God desires requires that we uncover the dirt and let God start cleaning up the mess.

"Why bother?" you say.

Answer: to set you free to love God, your family, your friends, and the whole world.

The fantastic news is that Jesus always stands ready to forgive us, no matter what we have done or how long we have been away from Him. That's what the Cross is all about: totally and completely cleaning up my sin on the outside and the inside.

> "The more fully we comprehend that the problem is sin, the more lovely the cross of Christ becomes."
> (Larry Crabb, *Inside Out* p. 33)

A young man named Evan Roberts heard a man speak one night at a church. This speaker, Seth Joshua, closed with the prayer: "Bend us, O God, bend us." Evan Roberts leaned over the chair in front of him and prayed: "Bend me, O God, bend me." He repented of his sin. God cleaned him up. Soon he began to speak to young people about what God had done. As a result of his repentance, God used him to start a mighty movement that swept all across England and America and brought hundred's of thousands of people to Christ.

➡ What do you think God could do through your repentant attitude? Dream a little.

• •

CALL ON THE HOLY SPIRIT TO GET FILLED UP.
A whole new engine, that's what Peter got. Changed from the inside out. Instead of operating by his own power, he had a new power.

Scared—that describes Jesus' disciples before the Resurrection. What clues does **John 20:19** give us that the disciples were afraid?

··

··

Then Jesus walked in the door. Fear disappeared.
Immediately He gave Peter and the disciples three gifts.

- Peace—"Peace be with you." (verse 21)
- Purpose—"As the Father has sent Me, I am sending you." (verse 21)
- Power—"Receive the Holy Spirit." (verse 22)

When the engine on my car went bad this year, I had only three choices:
1) Drive it over the cliff
2) Push it everywhere
3) Get a new engine
The car was too valuable to drive over the cliff. Pushing it everywhere seemed stupid because it defeated the purpose of having a car. So, I put in a new engine. Not only does my car run again, but now it runs like a new car. It has power it never had before.

People your age often don't see their value, so without Christ they "drive themselves over the cliff" doing things that destroy them. Others in the church try to live for Christ in their own power. That's as frustrating as trying to push your car everywhere. You have an engine, but you don't use it. The only intelligent move is to turn on the engine of the Holy Spirit in your life. That way you have the power you need to live the Christian life and to love your friends at school.

To put it another way, it is like breathing.

Physically, you have to breathe to stay alive and healthy. When you breathe, you exhale carbon dioxide and then inhale life-giving oxygen. Spiritually, the same is true. When you breathe spiritually, you exhale by confessing your sin. Then you inhale when you breathe in the Holy Spirit.

From **1 John 1:9** and **Ephesians 5:18** what do you discover about "spiritual breathing"?

• 1 John 1:9...

• Ephesians 5:18...

Learn to practice this every day, even many times during the day and the Holy Spirit will change you from the inside out.

One of the incredible results of the Holy Spirit changing and rearranging us on the inside is that He releases in us the power of the Holy Spirit to boldly tell our friends about Christ. Check out the promise of **Acts 1:8**. What promise does it make?

....

....

In high school I was scared to death to stand up in front of a group of people and talk. As president of the student body my senior year, I had to give speeches all the time. Every time I would write out every word on a 3 x 5 card, and with trembling hands and shaking knees, I would read the speech. Later, when I received Christ and He released His powerful Holy Spirit in me, He took away all of that fear and replaced it with boldness. Now I get the biggest rush out of speaking to young people about Christ. Only God's Spirit can make that kind of dramatic change.

Right now ask the Holy Spirit to release Himself in you, to change you and give you the character of Jesus.

Holy Spirit: I repent of my sin. I invite You now to fill me. Release Yourself in me. Give me your power so I can reflect the character of Jesus to everyone around me. In Jesus' name, Amen.

Pray this same prayer every day.

When the green flag drops at the Indianapolis 500™, thirty-three gleaming, low-slung turbocharged weapons will shoot out to the fourth turn and scream through the starting gate at almost 200 miles per hour.

But give the race a little time, and as in past years, the toll will start to be taken. Accidents, tire problems, gearbox failure, and a host of other calamities will wipe out many cars so that only half of the cars will finish the race.

On the pace lap, and even on the first few racing laps, every car looks invincible. But the goal is not to start well, it is to finish well. Trophies don't get handed out to those who cross the starting line. Rather the prize and the money go to those who cross the finish line.[2]

Your car is in the race! Keep it clean through repentance and keep it filled with the Holy Spirit. Then God will use you to make a difference with your friends and in your school over the long haul. Stay in the race!

(Note: the above comes from Andy Stanley, Barry's pastor, from his message on "Renewing Your Mind.")

* * * * *

I have invited the Holy Spirit to continually take control of every area of my life.

*Signed*_____

NOW GET READY FOR PASSIONATE
ROMANCE WITH GOD

---

[1] From a message preached by Andy Stanley, First Baptist Church North, Atlanta, Georgia.

[2] Bill Hybels, "The Character Crisis," Preaching Today, Tape #57

CHAPTER 5

Passionately Romantic

"The man who kneels to God
can stand up to anything." (*Anonymous*)

Guys, do you remember the first time you called a girl you liked on the phone? (Or maybe you are still trying to screw up your courage to do that!) Remember how hard it was. You thought about it for days. Finally, you decide you would call no matter what. You pick up the phone and start to dial. Then your hands start to shake. You hang up the phone. After several tries, you finally let the phone ring. She answers. You hyperventilate. She hears this heavy breathing and hangs up. After you get your composure, you try again. Your mind goes blank, but you blurt out, "Hello, Mary, this is movies, will you go to the john with me."

➡ Guys, why are we so mental when it comes to talking with girls? List at least three opinions. (Ask some girls.)

1. ....

2. ....

3. ....

Girls, it seems that you were born to talk, especially on the phone. You have waited for days for this guy to call you. Every time the phone rings, and your little brother tries to answer it, you punch him in the stomach. Then you body slam him. Then you answer, ever so sweetly, "Hello, this is Mary....Oh, hi....I'm so glad you called....Oh, I'm spending some time with my sweet little brother." Nervously you talk nonstop for fifteen minutes!

➡ Girls, why is it so easy for you to talk on and on and on? List at least three opinions. (Ask some guys.)

1. ....

2. ....

3. ....

Let's say your phone conversation goes really well. After a few times on the phone, you both relax, and talk more easily. After a while you find yourself spending hours together on the phone. Why? The relationship is deepening. The deeper it goes the more you enjoy talking to each other! Now instead of being afraid to talk, you find it becomes intensely exciting.

"HAVE YOU EVER THOUGHT ABOUT BECOMING A **CHRISTIAN**, AND YOU HAVE THE **CUTEST EYES** AT WAKEMONT HIGH."

Your relationship to God is like that. At first you might find it hard to talk to God. In fact, if somebody called on you to pray out loud, you might just croak.

TALKING TO GOD SURVEY
On a scale of 1 to 10 give a number to each statement (1 = disagree 10= agree)

1 2 3 4 5 6 7 8 9 10

- Prayer is boring.

- Praying in groups
  makes me nervous.

- God answers my
  specific prayers.

- Praying makes
  me sleepy.

- Raising my hands in
  worship makes my
  pits sweat.

- I have a hotline
  to heaven.

UP CLOSE AND PERSONAL
You may be asking: "Why is prayer important for me to make a difference on my campus?" Simple answer: Unless you know Jesus up close and personal, you can't communicate Him to your friends.

The great people of the earth today are the people who pray. I do not mean those who talk about prayer; nor those who say they believe in prayer; nor...those who can explain about prayer; but I mean those people who take time and pray (S.D. Gordon).

The only way you will take your campus for Christ is to understand, in no uncertain terms, that it will happen only through prayer. That begins with the intimacy and romance of your personal prayer life.

Prayer is not:
- A rabbit's foot for good luck
- A vending machine to get a spiritual candy bar
- A Coke to get a spiritual caffeine high

Rather consider it the incredible privilege of spending time with the Creator of the universe who gave His life on the cross because He loves you so much.

> *My translator in Russia, Lena Ostapenko, a Julia Roberts look-alike, had come to know Jesus eighteen months before our team arrived. Spending time alone with God every day was a totally new thought to her. Hungry to know God, she decided that she would get up one hour early every day (even though she is not a morning person). "But," she confessed, "I don't know what to do or say." I gave her a copy of my book SPENDING TIME ALONE WITH GOD to help her. She cried. It's the only other Christian book she owns besides the Bible. She not only uses it for herself, but is teaching seven other young girls to pray as well. She considered getting with God a wonderful privilege.*

➡ How zealous are you to communicate with God every day?

Hot to	No big	Ice
trot	deal	cold

Count on this: God wants you so close to Him that He can tell you His deepest thoughts, and confide in you His most intimate secrets.

THE PASSION TO COMMUNICATE
If we look at the life of Jesus in the Gospels like a play, Jesus is the star, many others are in supporting roles, and prayer,

the passion to communicate with His Father, is the back-drop.

He began in prayer. Describe the dramatic way Jesus began His public ministry in **Luke 3:21-22.**

....

....

He continued in prayer. Luke tells us: "But Jesus often withdrew to lonely places and prayed" (Luke 5:16). Discover some of the other times Jesus prayed specifically before a big decision or event.

•Luke 6:12-13...

•Luke 9:16..

•Matthew 14:22-23..

•John 11:41-42...

He ended in prayer. From **Luke 22: 39-46** find out everything you can about how Jesus handled this crisis in the Garden of Gethsemane through prayer.

....

....

....

....

Then on the cross, He called out to God with a loud voice: "Father, into Your hands I commit My spirit." (Luke 23:46)

He keeps on praying. Check out **Hebrews 7:25** to find out when Jesus prays for you and what the result is.

....

> "The Lord Jesus is still praying. Thirty years of living, thirty years of serving, one tremendous act of dying, 1,900 years of prayer. What an emphasis on prayer."
> (S.D. Gordon)

Jesus had a passion to pray. That's because He knew that everything hinged on His communication with His Father.

Jesus wants us to have the same kind of passion to communicate with His Father that He had. Jesus offers us the privilege of passionate prayer as a gift. He gives that just like a guy gives a girl flowers. It's a signifcant part of a special relationship.

A LOVE NOTE

Along with the flowers (or a boutonniere for the guys), He has written you a "love note" letting you know how exciting communication with Him can be. Have you ever written a love note and then had it trashed? Heart Break City! Jesus wants you to read His love note, and take it seriously.

The whole Bible is His "Love Book" to you. And one of the little notes inside it goes like this.

> *I tell you the truth, anyone who has faith in Me[that's you] will do what I have been doing. [preaching the Good News, healing the sick, delivering those oppressed by Satan] He will do even greater things than these, [wow!] because I am going to My Father. And I will do whatever you ask in My name [answer your prayer], so that the Son may bring glory to the Father. You may ask Me for anything in My name, and I will do it. [what a promise!] (Jesus in John 14:12-14)*

If He wrote it, He'll do it!

He comes through on what He promised you in that "love note" by answering you when you talk to Him. Just to give

66

you an idea of how dramatically and powerfully God does that, check this out.

After my Dad discovered that he had cancer, three doctors told him to go home, because there was nothing to do. It was terminal. I was in one of those meetings where the doctor put the X-rays on the wall and showed my Dad the cancer spots all over his spine.

I, along with the rest of my family, began to pray for my dad every day. One morning in church the Lord gave me a picture in my mind. I saw my dad's x-rays on the wall with all the spots. Then I saw this Big Hand with a dart gun in it. (The kind that shoots the rubber darts that you used when you were a kid.) This big hand was shooting these rubber darts at the black cancer spots. The dart would stick then drop to the floor peeling off the black cancer spots. It kept shooting and peeling until all of the spots were gone. I'm thinking: "That's really wierd!"

Our family had a special time of prayer for my dad about a week later. During the night he said that "The Lord woke me up and did something unusual in my body." Later, when he finished his cancer treatments and the doctor looked at the x-rays his exact words were, "It looks like those cancer spots on your spine have peeled right off of there."

Alcoholics set free, homosexuals delivered, people with physical and emotional abuse healed, a couple's relationship destroyed by an affair restored, kids on drugs released, pregnant teenagers helped, all by releasing God's resources through passionate prayer.

Prayer
Releases
All
Your
Eternal
Resources

➡ Reflect, when has God answered your prayers? Write down three or four.

....

....

....

....

➡ Right now, why don't you write a love note back to Him expressing your desire to talk to Him.

Dear God...

MAKING PLANS FOR THE BIG DATE

"Yeah, prayer sounds great, but I don't have a clue about what to do. Help!" OK! What did Jesus do in **Mark 1:35?**

....

What He did is exactly what you need to do!

Get up. That's the first big move. You will have all kinds of excuses for not getting up, not the least of which is, "I'm not a morning person. Can't I do this at night?" The reason you are a night person is that you stay up at night. The reason you are not a morning person is that you don't get up in the morning. If you make a habit of getting up you will become a morning person. (A miracle, no less.)

Besides, no team warms up after the game. God wants you to warm up with Him before the action of your day begins.

> One student made a commitment to God to get up in the morning. But he struggled with it. He hated getting up. Setting his alarm clock did not help. Determined, he set up a contraption that insured him of getting up. To his alarm clock he attached a fishing pole that hung over his bed. The fishing line hung down with four hooks. Each hook was connected to one corner of his covers. When the alarm went off the fishing rod reeled in the blanket! Not only did he get up and get with God, he became an influential spiritual leader on his campus, and later on throughout the country.

Radically ridiculous! Are you willing to become like that in order to have personal communication time with God?

Choose a time. Select a time that will give you 20–30 minutes with God in the morning. (That probably means you need to go to bed 20–30 minutes earlier.)

➡ Time I will meet with God every day:.......................

Find a quiet place. Your next major step is to find a place where you can be alone. Notice that when Jesus got up He "left the house." You may or may not need to do that. The point is to find a place alone where you won't be distracted by your parents or brothers and sisters. One of my friends tried several places and finally settled on the bathtub. Think of a good place for you to meet with the Lord.

➡ Place I will meet with God every day:.......................

Focus your attention. Your final step of preparation is to focus your attention. You can't do that if you are still half asleep. Get a shower. Get dressed. Don't forget to brush your teeth. Oh, yeah, and floss too! Turn on some Christian music. Get your Bible, preferably the *New International Version,* and a notebook, preferably a *Time Alone with God Notebook.* Consider this a "date" with God. Pray this prayer: "Lord, I'm here and I want to talk with You." Now count on Him to meet you.

➡ Preparation I will make to meet with God every day:

....

....

GOING OUT IN STYLE

Just like talking with someone special on the phone, talking with God is two-way communication. One person never dominates the conversation. If that happens, then talking gets boring. So how do you carry on this two-way conversation?

GOD TALKS, YOU LISTEN.

The reason God gave you only one mouth, but two ears is so you can listen twice as much as you talk.

One man I met could stand outside at night and hear the sounds of 500 different kinds of crickets! He had a PhD. in crickets! We need to train our spiritual ears to hear the voice of God like that guy could hear crickets.

➡ We listen to God by reading His Word and then letting Him speak to us. **Hebrews 4:12** tells us that when we listen, "the Word of God is living and active...it penetrates." What part of you does God's Word livingly, actively penetrate? (See the verse.)

••

••

- Start with John 1:1-5 then read one paragraph in John every day.
- Make your own copy of the BIBLE RESPONSE sheet from page 114.

(NOTE: *The Time Alone with God Notebook* will have numerous copies of this sheet in it, plus other helpful information. Order from the address in the front of the book or your local Christian bookstore.)

YOU TALK, GOD LISTENS.

You will never get a busy signal or get put off by "Call Waiting" when you talk to God. He is very interested in hearing from you. His "ears are attentive to your prayers" (1 Peter 3:12). He has already left you a message to call Him.

Often after we "bless Mom and Dad" and say "Give me a good day," we run out of things to say unless, of course, we have a big test. But **Hebrews 4:16** tells us how to approach God. How do we do that?

71

....

....

➡ Use these instructions to help you in your prayer time:
- Praise—Expressing to God how much you appreciate His awesome character qualities.
- Confession—Admitting your sins to God honestly.
- Thanksgiving—Telling God how grateful you are for all He has given you.
- Petition—Asking God for what you need.
- Intercession—Praying for others including your friends, family, and people who need to know Christ.

➡ Make a copy of the PRAYER ACTION sheet on page 116.

(NOTE: *The Time Alone with God Notebook* will have numerous copies of this sheet.)

Will you begin the habit of "going out" with God?

Because I want to get to grow in my passion for God, I agree to have a daily time alone with God
at ....(place) and at ....(time)
for ....days.
Signed...
Date..

PRAYER IS THE LAUNCH PAD FOR THE MISSILE OF THE HOLY SPIRIT TO STRIKE POWERFULLY ANY-PLACE IN THE WORLD, WITH NO DEFENSE AGAINST IT.

GETTING ENGAGED
Have you ever encountered a girl who just got engaged? Her "man" has captured her heart and she has captured his.

She walks around with her ring finger in everyone's face so all can see "the ring." He just walks around grinning like the cat that ate the mouse. They are captivated by the exciting adventure of growing more in love every day. They are in love. And everybody knows it.

In a romance with Jesus Christ, God will capture your heart. He will become your love. Growing in love with Him will get to be the most exciting adventure of your life. And when it is, you will want everyone to know it, especially your friends at school!

* * * * *

I commit myself to spending time alone with God every day for at least 15 minutes.

*Signed*_____

NOW GET READY TO PRAY FOR YOUR CAMPUS

CHAPtER 6

Ultimately
the Power Weapon

"There is a battle going on all over the world,
which is, in the final analysis,
a battle for the hearts, minds and souls of men and women."[1]

All kinds of weird things happen in the halls at school. Some are humorous.

▷A senior superglues a freshman's locker shut.

▷Every sophomore decides to park his or her gum on one cheerleader's math book.

▷The food fight in the cafeteria strategically targets the homecoming queen.

▷Your biology teacher confesses what you suspected: the frog guts from the biology lab have been used by the cafeteria staff to make the "mystery meat."

But some are not so humorous. What if a 250-pound senior tackle on the football team threatened to stuff your body into a locker? Not funny!

If you are a 150-pound freshman, you are shaking in your sneakers. Unless, of course, you have a black belt in karate. In that case the 250-pound tackle would occupy three different lockers with three sections of his body and he would pay rent for the space!

➡ What makes a 250-pound bully so scary?.....................

➡ What makes a 150-pound freshman so scared?............

....

➡ In your opinion what difference does a black belt in karate make?..

Satan is like that 250-pound tackle. He pushes around pretty much everyone at your school, possibly including you. It seems like everyone is like the 150-pound freshman getting stuffed into the locker. They don't even put up a fight. "Why bother? I'd just get clobbered."

But wait! You're no wimp! You may not look too strong or act very powerful sometimes. But you are armed with Jesus and His power.

➡ When you hang around your locker every day how do you see yourself? Circle one.
Mega wimp/Semi wimp/No clue/White belt/Brown belt/Black belt

➠ Why do you see yourself that way?............................

....

> "In Jesus, I'm Satan's Personal Nightmare!"
> —Quoted from a T-shirt owned by my teenage son.

➠ Do you see yourself as Satan's personal nightmare?_____

You are in a battle between the power of evil and the power of God.

Let's see what it's like on both sides of the battle lines.

THE POWER OF EVIL

Who is the enemy and what is his strategy at your school?

➠ To begin, make a list of all the negative junk that people at your school are into, including your friends.

....

....

Please understand that these things are NOT the problem. They are only the symptoms. Attacking these things and the people who do them will never change anything or anyone! Behind all of this is the Evil One.

- Satan is not an abstract principle or force, but a personality who works through people.
- The scientific world dismisses him a figment of imagination, which cannot be proved.
- People make fun of him as a harmless figure with a red suit, horns, a tail, and a pitchfork.
- The Bible describes him as Satan, Lucifer, Beelzebub, the Prince of the Power of the Air, the Prince of this World, the Father of Lies.

- He talks, thinks, acts, quotes the Bible, and then lies about it.
- He is the author of disease, death, evil, and fear.
- He poses as an "angel of light." Attractive and beautiful, he tempts you and your friends. He promises to satisfy, but he is dangerous and destructive.
- He has a strategy: to destroy God's purpose for your life.

What Satan does can be as simple as causing you to feel depressed, or as devastating as destroying another person's life.

 The Apostle Peter best expressed how Satan operates in **1 Peter 5:8.** What's his point?

••

Yes, Satan is powerful. Lots of times it seems like he has control of everything on your campus, including you. You probably feel like he is devouring you—eating you for lunch! In spite of that God has called you to push back the power of evil and to bring in the power of God.

THE POWER OF GOD
Jesus wants to defeat Satan at your school. He wants to do it by His power working through you! And He wants to do it with prayer!

> "The main concern of the devil is to keep the saints from praying. He fears nothing from prayerless studies, prayerless work, prayerless religion. He laughs at our toil, he mocks our wisdom, but he trembles when we pray." (Samuel Chadwick)

Terry and I had several conversations on the bus and in the "smoking circle." He had come with 300 other students to a week-long Raft Rally. We had fun whitewater

78

rafting during the day and then meeting at night to talk about Jesus Christ. Most were not believers. By Wednesday Terry had decided he wanted to follow Christ, and he was very sincere.

That's why I was so surprised two days later when he was causing a big disturbance in the camp. The youth leader talked to him. After a few minutes the youth leader realized he needed help. When I walked in and I could see why. Terry, normally a very nice guy, was growling and glassy-eyed. He looked wild and was threatening us. Then he started talking in a gutteral voice. It didn't take a spiritual giant to see that Satan had a foothold in his life.

It was easy to see why. He had a Ouija board that he used all the time. He fed himself a steady diet of heavy metal music, Dungeons and Dragons, sex, and drugs. His mom, obsessed with death, read constantly from the stacks of books in their house on that subject.

We prayed for Terry. Speaking in Jesus' name, we identified the demons that were afflicting him, then we demanded that they get out and leave Terry.

They did. He walked out of that room a free man. Through prayer we took back from Satan what belonged to God. The power of God overcame the power of evil.

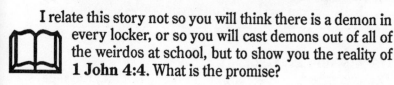 I relate this story not so you will think there is a demon in every locker, or so you will cast demons out of all of the weirdos at school, but to show you the reality of **1 John 4:4**. What is the promise?

•••

Try this logic:
- Satan is more powerful than you are.
- Jesus is more powerful than Satan.
- Jesus lives in you.
- Therefore, you are more powerful than Satan!

> You can break Satan's strong-hold in the lives of your friends and over your school. "How?" you say. THROUGH POWERFUL PRAYER!

After Peter does his bit about Satan as the "roaring lion," he describes in **1 Peter 5:6** how God will use you in that spiritual battle.

In the battle at school every day, what does this verse tell you about where you get the power to make a difference?

....

As you call on His power, what does He promise He will do for you?

1................................... 3......................................

2................................... 4......................................

> John Wesley, leader of the First Great Awakening: "Give me 100 men who fear nothing but sin and desire nothing but God...such alone will shake the gates of hell and set up the Kingdom of Heaven on earth."

THE WINNING STRATEGY

The triangle is the strongest geometric unit. Engineers build buildings, bridges, and roads with the basic design of the triangle. God set it up that way in the physical world as well as in the spiritual world.

> "The most powerful form of energy we can generate is not mechanical, electronic, or atomic, but prayer energy. When we pray we link ourselves with the inexhaustible power that binds the universe."
> Alexis Carrel, one of America's foremost scientists.

What does **Jeremiah 33:3** (note the triangle here—3,3,3) say to you about praying for you school?

....

....

Promise / \ Power

Pray

- PRAY—"Call to Me." Nothing will happen with your friends or your school until you get off your duff and spend time calling out to God. He is waiting for you to do that.

- PROMISE—God promises to respond: "I will answer you." When you pray, God moves into action.

- POWER—When God answers, He goes all out to show you great and mighty things"—things beyond your wildest imagination.

The youth group drove from Colorado into Wyoming on a mission trip traveling in a bus and two vans. At night, one of the vans hit an icy spot on the mountain road. The car flipped over twice as it plummeted down the side of the mountain. Amazingly, except for minor scratches, everyone seemed OK...until they could not find the six-year-old girl. Searching in the dark, they found her twenty minutes later, pinned under the van. She was unconscious, and crushed. Using CPR, they helped her to breathe until the ambulance arrived.

At the hospital they discovered the girl had a broken back, collapsed lungs, and a brain hemorrhage. The doctors told the group "She's not going to make it. And if she does she will be a vegetable." Already the students had begun to pray for her. With every negative report they prayed more boldly for God to heal her. They prayed all night.

The next morning the doctors at this smaller hospital decided to fly her to Salt Lake City for better treatment. The youth group stayed and prayed. On the flight she regained conscousness. She walked off the plane under her own power. At the hospital the doctors could find absolutely nothing wrong with her! *No broken bones. No collapsed lungs. No brain damage. All of her injuries had been documented by x-rays at the other hospital. But now, nothing!*

God chose in a miraculous way to demonstrate His power. He did it in answer to the prayers of these students. When and how He chooses to do that, I don't have a clue. But I do know this: He would do so much more if we called on Him to do more. He wants to answer you and demonstrate His power on your behalf.

THE PRAYER TRIANGLE: A POWER TEAM

Jesus challenges you to become a part of the Prayer Power Team in **Matthew 18:18-20.** How does it work and what are the results?

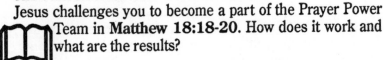

When we pray in groups of two and three He comes into the group and makes His presence and power available to us. Then He sends us out in His name to be the answer to our own prayers. Incredible!

"So how do I get this going?" you ask. "I really want to see God work in the lives of my friends." Here's how.

3 Friends
Meeting 3 Times a Week to Pray
For 3 Friends Who Need Christ

• **3 Friends**
➡ Write your name and two of your Christian friends' names at your school with whom you would like to pray.

How fantastic to know that at least two other people will be praying for you and with you regularly.

• Meet 3 Times a Week to Pray

➡ Write in the circles the three best times for you to pray, then confirm that with your other two friends.

You can arrange your schedule however you want. You can meet before school, between class, during a free period, at lunch, after school, at night, on the weekend. You can even meet over the phone. You get the idea. Work it out together. Flex with it, if needed. Just make sure you get 10–15 minutes together when you meet. Don't feel like you have to pray for everything every time. When it is time to go, go, knowing that you will be back together real soon.

• For 3 Friends Who Need Christ

➡ Now write the names of three friends who need Christ.

Use the space around the circles to describe their spiritual situation and to write down specifically what you want to pray for them.

When your group meets together, you are asking God to change the lives of 9 of your friends. If that happens you will already have a small spiritual revolution on your campus. And my guess is that it probably will.

During my son Scott's junior year in high school, he started a prayer triangle with his friends. They met in a classroom and in the bleachers on the football field. Over the spring semester here's what happened.

His friend, Teague, who had not been to a Fellowship of Christian Athletes meeting all year, showed up. That night the speaker gave an opportunity to accept Christ. Teague did.

Chris was struggling with the constant battle between his divorced parents, and burdened by his sister's problems. One night in his room, frustrated with life, he cried out to God. Right there, with no one around, he opened his heart to Christ.

Robert, Scott's Jewish friend, came up to him in the weight room one day and asked: "Scott, did Jesus die for me?" (That's a pretty significant question for a Jewish boy to ask!) What followed was a 20-minute discussion about the Gospel. Then Robert asked: "Scott, do you ever pray for me?" Scott said "Yes, every day." With misty eyes, Robert said: "Keep it up. I need your prayers."

For tips on how to start a prayer power team of your own, see page 118 in the back of the book.

THE PRAYER POWER TEAM CHALLENGE
Imagine! Your Prayer Power Team begins to see God work in your friends' lives. Other Christians in your school or youth group decide they want to begin a Prayer Power Team. Soon the power of God is popping all over your campus. People begin to accept Christ. The Christian groups begin to have enthusiasm and life. The momentum builds. More people come to Christ. Everybody knows something is happening. Now you have a Prayer Power Movement.

Take it one step further. Let's say that every one who reads this starts a Prayer Power Team on their campus. And the same thing happened to them that is going to happen to you. Can you imagine? A Prayer Power Movement would take place on campuses all over this country. A student prayer movement like this can change your generation. And it all begins with you! Will you take the challenge?

* * * * *

I will begin a Prayer Power Team with
     Me...
     Friend #1..
     Friend #2..
I will meet 3 times a week at
     Time #1..
     Time #2..
     Time #3..
I will pray for these friends who need Christ
     Friend #1..
     Friend #2..
     Friend #3..

*Signed*_____

NOW GET READY TO SERVE YOUR FRIENDS

[1] Douglas Hyde, Dedication and Leadership, (Notre Dame Press)

CHAPTER 7

Intensely Loving

"Preach the gospel all the time.
If necessary, use words."
Francis of Assisi [1]

Your life is the only Bible most people ever read," the saying goes. If that saying is true, then what do people come away with after they "read" you?
(Check the appropriate one)

❏ An earful
❏ An upset stomach
❏ A headache
❏ Less money
❏ A pain in the rear

❏ A smile
❏ A word of encouragement
❏ A helping hand
❏ A listening ear

❏ Other...

The story goes that during an inner city riot, the bombing, looting, and destruction created havoc in the neighborhood. A young girl woke up in the night frightened by all the noise. Realizing that her mother was still at work, she found herself all alone. That made her even more afraid, and she began to cry. Finally her mother did arrive home finding her little girl beside herself with fear. When she calmed down, she asked her mother, "Where were you?" Her mother said, "I know you were afraid, but remember, Jesus was here with you." The little girl angrily replied, "But mamma, I needed someone with skin on."

Jesus with skin on. That's who the people at your school need to see. They need for you to be "Jesus with skin on."

In an informal survey call three of your friends and find out how they came to know Christ. How many of them told you that someone who cared about them led them to Christ?

�!➡ Record their answers here.

1. ....

2. ....

3. ....

In Jesus' encounter with a leper in **Matthew 8:1-4,** four characteristics of Jesus' ability to love "with skin on" leap out at us and encourage us to love the way He did. When you read that story, what jumps out at you about being "Jesus with skin on" at your school?

....

....

So, tapping into His love, how do you become "Jesus with skin on" at your school?

I. PAY THE PRICE.
Large crowds followed Jesus. Even though they pressed in on Him and pressured Him, they never determined His response to people. To love others first determine to be different from the crowd.

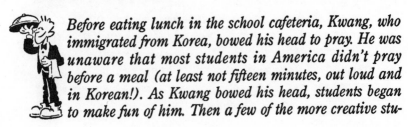 *Before eating lunch in the school cafeteria, Kwang, who immigrated from Korea, bowed his head to pray. He was unaware that most students in America didn't pray before a meal (at least not fifteen minutes, out loud and in Korean!). As Kwang bowed his head, students began to make fun of him. Then a few of the more creative stu-*

dents started to throw food at him. As a group of guys surrounded Kwang and teased him, Scott stepped in between them. He said, "This is my friend Kwang. I think you should stop making fun of him." The guys walked away—but not without a few choice comments about Scott being a geek for hanging around Kwang. It didn't really matter, because Scott understood that loving the way Jesus loved involves paying a price.

➠ Can you do what Scott did, putting your reputation on the line for someone else?

➠ How would you respond when someone drops his tray in the lunchroom?
- Point and laugh like a hyena until you bust a gut.
- Drop your tray on his, so he will have to pick up yours too.
- Gather a crowd and teach him some tray-handling drills.
- Help him pick it up, even the mushy smelly asparagus.

89

Jesus calls us "the light of the world." To widen your circle of influence with your friends and your school, you must understand that light opposes darkness. Therefore loving others will usually oppose what the majority does.

2. INCLUDE EVERYONE.

The man with leprosy came and knelt before Jesus. That was bad. The entire crowd scattered. You would think somebody telephoned in a bomb threat. That's because leprosy was the most dreaded disease in Jesus' day. It was like having AIDS today. People considered lepers as good as dead. Everyone avoided them. Lepers couldn't even live in the town. If one came close, people had to yell "Unclean! Unclean!" That way people could avoid contact with them. "Only the Lonely" was the leper's theme song.

In your school some people get treated as lepers. They may not have a disease or have to yell "unclean," but people avoid them "like the plague" in order to protect their reputations. These "lepers" won't increase your popularity rating but, without a doubt, they are the people Jesus would come to first if He visited your school.

Chris was such a person. He never knew his dad. He lived with his mother and grandmother. Every day he went to school by himself, to class by himself, walked the halls by himself and ate lunch by himself. As the manager of the football team, He listened to football players yell at him for two hours every day. Then he went home and spent the evening with his mother and grandmother. The phone never rang and he never went out with friends. Chris wasn't "with it." He had no dynamic personality, no Tom Cruise smile, no party animal. Chris was just Chris.

"If you love those who love you, what credit is that to you? Even 'sinners' love those who love them...but love your enemies."
Jesus
Luke 6:32,35

➡ Who falls in the "least loved" category at your school? Name one person in each of the following categories:

▷"The Leper": the one made fun of or avoided because he is not popular or does not look a certain way.

··

▷"Zacchaeus": the one who takes advantage of others, but is really insecure.

··

▷"The Adulterous Woman": the one who has rumors follow her all over school.

··

▷"The Samaritan Woman": the one from a different background, race, nationality, or social status.

··

Jesus loved these kinds of people. When you love the kinds of people Jesus loved, you express the compassion of Jesus.

3. TOUCH PEOPLE'S LIVES

The plot thickens in the story of the leper as Jesus continues to break all of the social rules. As the crowd scatters for fear of catching the dreadful disease, the leper looks into the eyes of Jesus and asks Jesus to help him. As if the leper were the only one in this large crowd, Jesus reached out and "touched the man" (Matthew 5:13).

I seriously doubt that Jesus just barely touched him with the tips of His fingers. No. Most likely He put His arms around the leper and hugged him, just so he would know how "lovely" he was to Jesus. Years had passed since the leper had felt the touch of another person. That's radical love!

> Love looks beyond unlovable characteristics,
> to give a big hug in Jesus' name.

To express God's love may mean we get hurt, rejected, misunderstood, or taken advantage of. Yet we keep on loving even when everyone else has stopped. We decide before the fact, that we will love, no matter what responses we encounter.

> *For two years a small group of students reached out to Chris. Every week they invited him to a meeting, and every week he promised to come. But he never showed up. Sometimes the group got discouraged but never gave up. They keep loving Chris even when no one else cared, even Chris himself.*

➡ Honestly evaluate how you would respond to the following situations:

1. A friend of yours starts a rumor that you had sex with your date Friday night.

....

2. Someone smacks you in the back of the head during algebra class.

....

3. Your English teacher accuses you of cheating on an exam and gives you a zero.

....

4. The most unpopular student in the school asks you for a ride home from school.

....

5. The bully of the school pokes his finger in your favorite dessert.

....

Now take each situation and describe how you think Jesus would have responded to each person.

1. Your "friend"

....

2. The mad head-smacker

....

3. Ms. "I'll catch you even if you didn't do it"

....

4. The guy most likely to destroy your cool "rep"

....

5. The dangerous dessert destroyer

....

Baron Von Kamp lived in Prussia (Germany). A Christian and very wealthy, he used most of his wealth to give the poor jobs and to serve others in the name of Christ. Also he helped many students with their college education. One such person was Thomas, an atheist. Von Kamp opened his home to him and paid for his education. When Thomas came home every evening, the Baron went to meet him so he could serve him in any way. He even helped him take off his boots. Thomas tried to argue with him and make him look foolish. One night in an outburst Thomas said "Baron, how can you do all this? You see I do not care about you. How are you able to continue to be so kind to me and serve me like this?

The Baron replied, "My dear young friend, I have learned it from the Lord Jesus. I wish you would read through the gospel of John. Good night." That night Thomas trusted Christ. [2]

When you make a conscious decision to touch the lives of "the untouchables," then you become an unusual person whose circle of influence will penetrate the lives of many people at your school and beyond.

4. SERVE PEOPLE'S NEEDS.

God's love actively meets the practical needs of people. Jesus met the immediate physical need of the leper before He met his spiritual need. Jesus put a high priority on serving others and meeting their needs as evidence of His love.

In **Mark 9:33-35** the disciples had an argument about who was the greatest. What did Jesus tell them?

As the students in the group began to build a relationship with Chris, they looked for opportunities to serve him. They noticed that at the football games he was responsible for taping all the players, setting up all the equipment, filling all the water coolers, and making sure the players had cups of water. When the games were over and everyone else was either laughing (if we won) or crying (if we lost), Chris hung out in the dressing room cleaning up everyone's messy equipment. Seeing the situation and wanting to serve Chris, different ones in the group came early to the games to help Chris with his chores. They stayed after to help clean up the mess.

Serving and sharing God's love go hand in hand.

These ideas will help you serve your friends. Add three of your own at the end. Circle two you will use this week.

- ☐ Share a ride to school or other school events.
- ☐ Offer to give up the front seat when cruising.
- ☐ Offer to take a lunch tray back.
- ☐ Help pick up books someone has dropped.
- ☐ Get the class assignment for someone who is sick.
- ☐ Give your possessions freely: CDs, food, little brother (check with your parents on that last one!).
- ☐ Defend those others pick on.
- ☐ Include a lonely person in your circle of friends.
- ☐ Invite someone home for dinner (after you ask your parents).
- ☐ Offer to help with studies. (Will that help anyone?)
- ☐ Let others in front of you in line.
- ☐ Compliment someone on something he does well.
- ☐ Be available to talk to a hurting friend.
- ☐ Speak positively when someone is being cut down.

☐ ....

☐ ....

☐ ....

After two years of serving Chris with no apparent spiritual interest, he surprised the group by showing up at our meeting. That night he accepted Christ. Later he explained what happened.

"Life has always been kind of lonely and sad for me. I never had a dad and I never had many friends either. For the last two years I spent most of my time alone. Every day, without much contact with others, I would go to school, go to class, go to practice, and then go home to spend the evening with my mother and grandmother. I began to think this was pretty much the way life was going to be. Then you guys invited me to come here. The truth is I've never experienced so much love. I asked Christ into my life the other day. I never thought I could be so full.... You know the coffee commercial 'filled to the brim and overflowing', that's what I feel like now."

After Chris said this, Brent, one of the football players who had reached out to Chris, gave him one of the biggest bear hugs you have ever seen.

Today Chris is finishing his college education and preparing to be a pro football trainer for the Cleveland Browns (Why the Browns, I don't know!). His mission in life is to express the love of Christ to the football players he serves every day. He can do that because he will never forget how a group of people loved and served him.

Serving opens the door to communicate the life changing message of the Gospel.

➠ Name one person who is "unlovable" to you.

....

➠ Think of two creative ways you can serve him or her this week.

1. ....

2. ....

96

➡ Write out a prayer asking God to give you the strength and courage to love and serve as Jesus loved and served.

•••

•••

➡ Do this project with the other two people in your Prayer Power Team. Hold each other accountable for following through.

When you aggressively love other people, especially the "unlovely," then your reputation with your peers will be one of respect, whether they tell you that or not. When you show love by serving them, God will use you and your friends in an unusual way to have an ever-widening circle of influence with your entire school.

* * * * *

I will serve one person at my school who is hard to love.

*Signed*_____

NOW GET READY TO
BOLDLY SHARE CHRIST

[1]Charles W. Colson, The Body, (Dallas: Word Publishing, 1992) 88.
[2]George Müller, Edited by Diana L. Matisko, The Autobiography of George Müller (United States, Whitaker House, 1984), 135–138.

CHAPTER 8

Naturally Communicating

"The problem is not that students don't believe in Jesus, but that
they don't believe in anybody who believes in Jesus."
Jacob Aranza[1]

You go through the cafeteria line at school, eyeing the
"gobbledy-gook" they have billed as meatloaf. As you
walk to a table, you're dreaming of a burger, fries, and a
large Coke. When you sit down, you are jarred back into
reality by the conversations. Two guys are saying, "That girl
is a !@#$%^&* babe!" (and that's putting it mildly). Another
group is making plans for the "I Tappa Keg" drinking
blowout the next night. Still a third group is arguing over
the finer philosophical points of the latest "R" rated movie.
As a Christian you're sitting there listening to all of this
incredibly inane conversation by people you really care
about. How should you respond?

- ☐ Withdraw to a table of all Christians so you don't
  have to deal with this "worldly stuff."
- ☐ Slam your tray on the table, flipping the meatloaf into
  the lap of the girl across from you, and say, "Gross!
  God sends people to hell for stuff like that."
- ☐ Blow all circuits and get your Uzi out of your locker
  and send them all to hell right now.
- ☐ With boldness, courage, and sensitivity focus on one
  group or even one person, enter the conversation, and
  turn it to talk about Jesus Christ.

When I first met Tim, his pants sagged, his hair was half-

shaved, he had two earrings in both ears, and an attitude that said, "Get out of my face or I'll break yours." I learned that Tim was good with his hands, especially remodeling other kids' noses. Constantly fighting, he spent a good bit of his time on suspension from school.

After spending several months trying to get to know him, a wall still remained. He would not talk about anything serious, much less about Jesus Christ. I could sense the tension when Jesus was mentioned.

You probably have some relationships like that. While working with Tim I found in the story of Jesus and the woman at the well (John 4:7-42) some very powerful communication keys that helped me to unlock the door of Tim's life and express Christ to him.

Maybe they will help you unlock the doors of some of your friends' lives too. God wants to use you to reach into the lives of your friends. That will happen only when you know how to open the door of their lives with courage, boldness, and sensitivity.

LOCKER OPENER #1
        INITIATE RELATIONSHIPS.

Have you ever noticed that Jesus' life was filled with significant conversations with others? He had a way of getting people to talk about the personal issues in their lives.

Look at **John 4:6-7** to discover why people opened up to Christ.

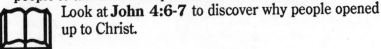

Even though He was hot and tired, Jesus took the initiative in friendship. He didn't wait for the woman to speak to Him. He spoke to her. Without speaking the first time, He would never have been able to continue the conversation. He opened the door by being friendly Himself.

> *With Tim, I had to initiate the relationship. He never would have. As I spent more and more time with him, he gradually opened up. At first he wouldn't talk much at all. But as I continued to be his friend, he gave me little glimpses into his life. Then one day through tears he shared he was thinking about killing himself. We talked. From that day on we could talk openly about anything.*

To open the door for a real relationship with another person try these "friend builders."

1. TAKE TIME.

To be a friend you have to give time. That usually means taking time away from what you would do for yourself.

- Block out specific times in your schedule to spend time with your friend.
- Do something he likes to do.
- Don't give up if it doesn't work out at first. Keep trying.

2. LISTEN.

People can tell if you are truly listening to them or not. Use these listening tips.
- Make eye contact.
- Focus on the other person, not on what you have to say.
- Ask clarifying questions like "How did you feel when that happened?" "What are you going to do now?"

3. HANG TOUGH.

Because of the pain, students want someone who cares enough to talk about the serious issues in their lives. They need someone who is concerned enough to hang in there. That's when they know they have a valued friend.

> People don't care how much you know
> until they know how much you care!

➡ Add to the following list two "pains" that your friends have experienced in the past year.

1. Parents splitting up.
2. Breakup with boyfriend or girlfriend.
3. Family member got sick.
4. Cut from a sports team.
5. Someone close dies.
6. Misunderstood by a teacher.
7. ....
8. ....

Try one or two of these personal questions to get past surface conversation and into the pain in your friend's life.

- I heard your parents might be breaking up; how are you doing with that?
- You've been absent from school lately. Are things OK?
- You seem a little down today. Anything going on that I can help you with?
- I know making that team meant a lot to you. If you would like to talk about it, I'm here.
- I heard you and Sally split up. How are you doing?

When you put some of these suggestions into action to initiate friendships, then you will make a significant difference in the lives of some people at your school.

LOCKER OPENER #2
COMMUNICATE LOVE AND ACCEPTANCE.

When a friend senses that you have more concern for getting his life right than for loving him, he will become defensive instead of hearing what you have to say.

That's not what Jesus communicated to the woman at the well. Jesus asked the Samaritan woman for a drink, disarming her, causing her to relax (John 4:7). And as the conversation proceeded, He communicated love and acceptance until she felt so comfortable that she said, "Give me this water so I won't get thirsty" (v. 15).

You can build an atmosphere of love and acceptance with your friends by using these suggestions.

1. DON'T EMBARRASS.
To avoid embarrassing a friend, use these tips.

- Ditch obnoxious Christian T-shirts like, "If you don't love Jesus, you're a dog eating vomit".
- Give him room to disagree with you.
- Be sensitive about what you say about his religion, even if it appears to be a cult.
- Realize that you don't have to win him to Christ every-time you see him.
- If someone else makes fun of him, come to his defense.

2. DON'T OFFEND.
Many times it is not the Gospel that offends, but our obnox-iousness. A "holier than thou" attitude turns people off quicker than having to go to summer school. So how can you avoid being an obnoxious Christian?

DON'T OFFEND

103

- Don't be "The Bible Answer Man," trying to give authoritative answers and a verse for every question.
- Don't be defensive when you don't know an answer.
- Don't argue when someone criticizes your beliefs.

Out of a heart of love for your friends, you can treat each one with dignity and respect. Realize that each one is created in the image of God. Through Christ, God wants to restore each one to His image. He will use you by inserting the key of love and acceptance to open that door.

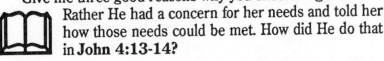

```
LOCKER OPENER #3
     RELATE CHRIST TO HIS
     PERSONAL NEEDS AND PROBLEMS.
```

Your friends want to know that there is hope for them in their personal needs and problems.

Jesus gave that kind of hope to the woman at the well. When Jesus talked with her, He didn't jump right in with, "Give me three good reasons why you shouldn't go to hell." Rather He had a concern for her needs and told her how those needs could be met. How did He do that in **John 4:13-14?**

···

···

One night in a discussion Tim told the group that his father had left his family a few years ago. He said he had assumed much of the responsibility for raising his little brothers and sister. Because he didn't have anyone to be a father to him, he was very lonely. We took that opportunity to talk with him about how God desires to be his Father, filling the "empty places" his earthly father had created.

The best way to share God's love is to relate how His love

meets needs. In Tim's case he needed a father.

➡ Identify one need that one of your non-Christian friends has now.

....

➡ Think of one practical way Jesus can help him or her with that need.

....

Everyone has personal needs and problems. They will surface soon enough. As you try to relate Jesus and His love to their needs, then God will use you to open the door of their hearts and let His love shine in.

```
LOCKER OPENER #4
        RELATE YOUR PERSONAL
        EXPERIENCE.
```

Your friends need to move from thinking about Jesus as external religion to understanding that He is internal reality. They need a picture of who God is. Jesus gives that to the woman in **John 4:13-14.** What does He tell her?

....

....

One of the best ways to do this is through communicating your own personal experience with Jesus.

With Tim we looked for opportunities to give him a picture of God through our lives. One day he talked about his concern for paying a speeding ticket due the next day. He was worried because he did not have the money. The

Lord impressed us that we were to help pay for the ticket. Initially Tim refused, saying, "You have bills of your own that you need to pay." This opened the door to tell him several personal experiences about how Christ had taken care of our needs.

Every Christian has a powerful personal testimony. Sometimes people feel that if they weren't drug addicts before they accepted Christ, their testimony is not valid. NOT! Your testimony is a picture of who God is in you, no matter what your background.

To become more effective in sharing your personal experience with God follow these helpful hints.

I. PREPARE YOUR TESTIMONY.

Answer these questions concerning your personal experience with Christ.

1. What major difficulty did you struggle with before you accepted Christ?

....

2. What key experience led you to Christ?

....

3. What specific difference has Christ made in helping you with the stuggle you mentioned in #1?

....

On page 120 you will find a worksheet to write your testimony. Focus on the points you wrote above in writing your testimony. Make sure you include one personal experience in each point.

☐ Check here when you have written your testimony.

Once you have written your testimony take time to memorize it and practice sharing it. You'll find tips for doing that on page 119 in the back of this book.

☐ Check here when you have memorized your testimony.

2. PRESENT YOUR TESTIMONY.

➡ Focus on one person you have prayed for who needs to know Christ. Get with that person this week and give your testimony. (See page 119 for helpful tips.)

☐ Check here when you have given your testimony to a friend.

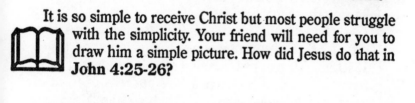

LOCKER OPENER #5
    SHOW HOW HE CAN KNOW
    GOD PERSONALLY.

It is so simple to receive Christ but most people struggle with the simplicity. Your friend will need for you to draw him a simple picture. How did Jesus do that in **John 4:25-26?**

••

••

One night Tim said to us "I want to have what you have." We weren't sure what he was talking about. I questioned him further. He replied, "Can you tell me how I can know the God I see in you?"

The door doesn't open any wider than that. At Hardees over a Coke and some curly fries I had had the privilege of introducing Tim to my friend, Jesus Christ.

It doesn't get any better than leading someone to Christ.

When you show someone how to know God, it is important that you draw him a clear picture. If you follow these suggestions, you can present the Gospel clearly.

1. TURN THE CONVERSATION.

Up to this point you have shared your personal experience. Now you will turn the focus of the conversation to your friend. To make that transition ask these questions.

- "Have you ever experienced a personal relationship with Jesus Christ like the one I've described?"
- "Would you be interested in knowing how to do that?"

> "Only one friend has ever said no to hearing the Gospel."
> (Keith)

2. COMMUNICATE THE MESSAGE CLEARLY.

You need to know what to say when the opportunity comes. Simply and clearly communicate the Gospel. You can do that by following these instructions.

- Use a booklet that clearly explains the Gospel. (A sample of *The Facts of Life* booklet is included on pages 121-126. You can order copies of this in booklet form from Reach Out Ministries [see address in front of book] or from your local Christian bookstore.)
- Memorize the main points of the booklet and the verses that go with each point.
- Read the booklet with him. Only use one booklet.
- Leave the booklet and your phone number with him.

3. ASK DISCERNING QUESTIONS.

Because you want him to actually know Jesus, not just pray a prayer, you need to ask these questions after you read through the prayer. These questions will determine your friend's level of understanding.

- "Do you understand what I just shared with you?"
- "What does this mean to you?"

Listen to the response. If he says something like, "I try to be good," or "I go to church every Sunday," or seems apathetic, you can be sure he hasn't grasped the real meaning of the Gospel. If he does understand, he will ask searching questions like:

- "How do I believe in Jesus Christ?"
- "How can I be sure He will come into my life?
- "Will Jesus forgive me my worst?"
- "Will Jesus take away the emptiness I feel?"

4. CHALLENGE TO ACCEPT CHRIST.

If you sense your friend has a clear understanding of the Gospel, then challenge him to receive Christ. Use the prayer on page 12 in the booklet.

Read the prayer out loud and then ask:

- "Does this prayer express the desire of your heart?"

If he says "yes," then lead him in the prayer to accept Christ. Have him pray the prayer out loud.

> After praying with Tim, I began to ask him if he understood all that I said. He nodded yes. Then I questioned him to make sure. He wanted Christ in his life and he wanted Him now. I led Tim in a prayer to receive Christ.

ASK DISCERNING
QUESTIONS

After he prayed he said, "This is the first time my heart has ever felt clean."

If he says "no" then follow through on the next step.

5. KEEP ON SHARING CHRIST
Those who don't accept Christ...
We can easily abandon those who reject our message. But there is no better way to share God's unconditional love with our friends than to remain a friend whether they respond or not.

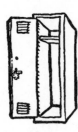

As I shared the love of Christ with Pete, he seemed very interested. I asked him if the prayer at the end of The Facts of Life *expressed his heart's desire. He was very polite. He told me that he respected what I had to say, but in no uncertain terms he told me, "I don't believe that God exists. And if there is no God, then there isn't any need for me to have a relationship with God." He had a point.*

So what do I do next? Maybe I could dust my Tevas off and pray down fire on his head! Instead I developed a plan to continue to love him and share Christ with him. Maybe some of the steps I took will help you.

- Don't get discouraged. Sharing Christ is a process.
- Continue to pray for him daily.
- Continue to serve him.
- Invite him to positive Christian events.
- Introduce him to other Christian friends.
- Give him books or booklets that relate to his struggles.
- Take time to answer his questions.

Those who do accept Christ...
When a friend accepts Christ, the responsibility has just begun. He is "like a newborn baby" (1 Peter 2:2). We have the privilege of helping him grow in his new faith.

A six session follow-up booklet entitled *Getting Started* is designed specifically for you to help your new Christian friend grow. It covers these issues.

1. "What happened when I accepted Christ?"
2. "How do I communicate with God?"
3. "How do I tell other people?"
4. "How do I get plugged in?"
5. "What happens when I mess up?"
6. "How will my life change?"

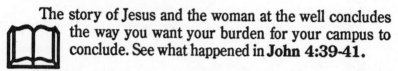 The story of Jesus and the woman at the well concludes the way you want your burden for your campus to conclude. See what happened in **John 4:39-41.**

Good news travels fast! The Samaritan woman couldn't contain herself. She had to share the love of God with others and it had a multiplying effect.

Remember Tim? Since he has accepted Christ, he has talked with a number of his friends about Christ. One was Pete. Once a total agnostic, Pete now meets with Tim every week.

God is continually in the process of bringing people to Himself. He allows you to enter into this incredible adventure! As you love God and your friends, God will cause you to become boldly unashamed of the Gospel. As you let the Gospel be the "power of God" in your own life, He will use you to influence more people than you can imagine! Possibly your entire campus!

To further develop your skills in communicating Christ to your friends look for *Giving Away Your Faith* by Barry St.Clair (Victor Books/Scripture Press), available at your local Christian bookstore.

HOW TO STUDY A PASSAGE OF SCRIPTURE

Follow these steps to make Bible study exciting. Use them on the BIBLE RESPONSE SHEETS.

Observe. (Use with the *Title* and *Key Verse* sections of the BIBLE RESPONSE SHEET.)
Pray first for the Holy Spirit's guidance, and then read the passage carefully. Read with an open mind, ready to receive and obey what God has to teach you.

Interpret. (Use with the *What does it say?* section of the BIBLE RESPONSE SHEET.)
Step One – Read the verses preceding and following the passage in order to understand the proper setting and context.
Step Two – Look up unfamiliar terms in a standard dictionary or a Bible dictionary.
Step Three – Outline the passage.

Apply. (Use with the *How does it apply to my life?* section of the BIBLE RESPONSE SHEET.)
Step One – Look for:

Promises to claim	Commands to obey
Attitudes to change	Actions to take
Challenges to accept	Examples to follow
Sins to confess	Skills to learn

Step Two – Describe how the passage applies to your life by asking yourself these questions:
- "How can I make this passage *personal*?"
- "How can I make it *practical*?"
- "How can I make it *measurable*?"

Be specific. For example: "I need to love my mom more by cleaning up my room every day."

Memorize (Use the *Memory verse* section of the BIBLE RESPONSE SHEET.)
Find a verse or passage of Scripture that speaks to you personally, and memorize it.

BIBLE RESPONSE SHEET

DAY/DATE _____

BIBLE PASSAGE _____

TITLE (Topic of Passage) _____

_____

KEY VERSE _____

WHAT DOES IT SAY? (Outline) _____

_____

_____

_____

_____

_____

_____

_____

_____

_____

_____

HOW DOES IT APPLY TO MY LIFE? _____

_____

_____

_____

_____

_____

_____

MEMORY VERSE _____

_____

BIBLE RESPONSE SHEET

DATE _5/10_

PASSAGE _John 1:1-5_

TITLE _Jesus brings light + life_

KEY VERSE _verse 4_

SUMMARY _the Word (Jesus)_
(1) was in the beginning,
(2) was with God, (3) was
God, (4) made all things,
(5) was life, and (6) was
light

PERSONAL APPLICATION _I need to let_
Jesus be who He wants to be
to me. I can experience His
life + light by spending 15
minutes alone with Him every
morning for the rest of this
series of studies.

PRAYER ACTION SHEET

DAY/DATE _____

PRAISE:
Write down one praise to the Lord today.

_____

_____

CONFESSION:
Write down any sin(s) you need to confess.

_____

_____

THANKSGIVING:
Write down what you are most thankful for today.

_____

_____

PETITION:
Write down any needs you have in your life today.

_____

_____

_____

INTERCESSION:
Write the names of the people you are praying for today and a phrase that expresses your prayer for each person.

Name   Prayer

_____   _____

_____   _____

_____   _____

_____   _____

_____   _____

PRAYING FOR OTHERS

 Through your prayers God will work powerfully in other people's lives. Pray for: your family, your Christian friends, friends who need Christ, your school, your church and the spread of the Gospel around the world. Be very specific in your requests.

Record your prayers on your PRAYER ACTION SHEET.

    Keep a record of the things you are praying for and write down God's answers to your prayers . Put in requests on each day of the week.

    Then pray for those requests on that day. Doing this will keep you from having too many requests on one day.

SUNDAY

Date Prayed	REQUEST	ANSWER	Date Answered
10/27	Mom — flu — relationship with sister	Mom — out of bed & feeling much better today	10/28
	Dad — new job — growth as Christian		
	Daniel — attitude toward me — girlfriend		
	Susan — grades — discipline — parents divorce	Susan — parents talking about getting back together	

SEVEN TOUGH QUESTIONS

These 7 Questions help me be honest about the dirt in my life and then confess it just like the Bible encourages me to do.

Spend at least one hour with these questions this week, then ask yourself one every day after that. Write down your responses on a separate sheet of paper.

---

7 QUESTIONS

1. Do you have impure thoughts about the opposite sex? (2 Timothy 2:22)

2. Do you gripe, complain, or have bad attitudes? (Philippians 2:14-15)

3. Do you respect, honor, and obey your parents? (Ephesians 6:1-3)

4. Do you lie, steal, or cheat? (Colossians 3:9)

5. Are bitterness and resentment keeping you from forgiving another person? (Matthew 6:14-15)

6. Have you treated another person wrongly? (Matthew 5:23-24)

7. Do you have any idols that keep Jesus from being first in your life? (Matthew 6:33)

- PURPOSE. Get clearly in your mind that your purpose is to PRAY. Make certain that your two Christian friends who will pray with you know the purpose.

- COMMITMENT. Ask your two friends point blank: "Will you join me three times a week to pray together?" Don't try to talk them into it if they are hesitant. If one decides not to, then ask someone else.

- TIME. Let your friends know that the length of time will vary, but the average time will be about 15 minutes each time. Decide to meet for 3 months. After that you can decide if you want to stop or go on.

- PLACE. Meet at school. Try to find a place that is reasonably quiet. Don't be afraid or ashamed to meet where others might see you.

- AGENDA. This simple structure will give you a guide to follow in your meetings. Spend about 5 minutes on each of these.

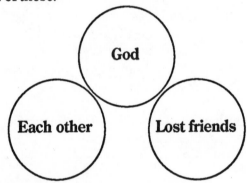

GOD. Worship God.
- Tell Him how great He is.
- Sing, read a psalm or other Scripture.
- Express thanks for what He means to you and what He has done for you.

EACH OTHER. Pray for each other.
- Pray that you will grow in your relationship to Christ.

- Be specific about needs that you have.
- Ask the Lord to make you a bold and sensitive witness on your campus.
- Pray foreach other's families and churches.

LOST FRIENDS. Ask the Lord to bring your friends to Himself.
- Ask the Lord to show you where your friends are spiritually. Ask Him to take them the next step.
- Each person pray for one friend, then each one go again until all 9 are prayed for. If you don't finish, then pick up where you left off next time.
- Pray for your campus too. Ask the Lord to bring a spiritual hunger to the principal, teachers, coaches, apathetic Christians, and lost students. Ask for the Gospel of Jesus Christ to be made known clearly to every person.

TESTIMONY TOOL AND TIPS
Use these pointers and the following sheet to write and share your testimony.
- Be Accurate—Don't try to "spice up" your testimony by stretching the truth. It will be the power of God that communicates His message.
- Be Personal—Use "I" and "me" a lot. People like to hear experiences told in the first person.
- Be Graphic—Be specific. Give enough details to arouse your listeners' interest.
- Be Thematic—Choose a central theme for your testimony that non- Christians can relate to (i.e., self esteem, security, purpose).
- Be Relaxed—Talk about your story as a natural part of the conversation without going into "pulpit mode".
- Honestly communicate your problems and difficulties.
- Be positive. Don't criticize others who believe differently than you.
- Use words that a non-Christian can relate to. Drop words like "saved," "sanctified," "washed in the blood."
- Focus on what Christ has done for you rather than on how bad your old life was.
- Talk as a friend, not like a preacher in a coliseum.

My Life Before I Met Christ

How I Met Christ

How Christ Has Changed My Life

BARRY ST. CLAIR

THE FACTS OF LIFE

Dates
FAMILY
POPULARITY
SCHOOL
PARTIES
Sex
SPORTS
MONEY
Clothes
Reputation

We look for meaning in life through these things. But the fact is — knowing God is more important than all these things put together. Why?

GOD LOVES US AND CREATED US TO KNOW HIM.

God loves us. Jesus said, "God so loved the world that He gave His one and only Son, that whoever believes in Him shall not perish but have eternal life" (John 3:16).

God created us. We read in the Bible. "For You (God) created my inmost being; You knit me together in my mother's womb" (Psalm 139:13).

God wants us to know Him. God's Word tells us, "Now this is eternal life; that they may know You, the only true God, and Jesus Christ, whom You have sent" (John 17:3).

4

MAN   **GOD**

Loves us
Created us
Wants us to know Him

Since Fact #1 is true, why is it that many people don't know God?

5

FACT 2

OUR SIN KEEPS US FROM KNOWING GOD.

Some people think of sin as getting drunk, or telling lies. True, but sin involves much more.

What is sin? Sin is our choice to disobey God and go our own way. "We all, like sheep, have gone astray, each of us has turned to his own way" (Isaiah 53:6).

Who has sinned? Everyone. In the Bible we read, "All have sinned and fall short of the glory of God" (Romans 3:23).

What happens when we sin? Sin results in separation from God, leading to death and judgment. "The wages of sin is death" (Romans 6:23), and, "Man is destined to die once, and after that to face judgment" (Hebrews 9:27).

As long as sin separates us from God, we cannot know Him.

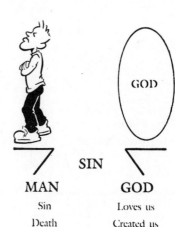

What, then, is the solution to our separation from God?

FACT 3

WE CAN KNOW GOD ONLY THROUGH JESUS CHRIST

Jesus Christ is the only solution to our sin problem.

Jesus died for our sin. "God demonstrates His love for us in this: While we were still sinners, Christ died for us" (Romans 5:8).

Jesus rose from the dead to give us life. "Just as Christ was raised from the dead through the glory of the Father, we too may live a new life" (Romans 6:4).

Jesus opened the way for us to know God. "For Christ died for sins once for all, the righteous for the unrighteous, to bring you to God" (1 Peter 3:18).

The life, death, and resurrection of Jesus Christ bridged the gap from God to us.

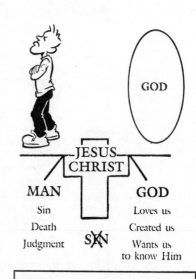

How can we know Jesus Christ personally?

FACT 4

TO KNOW GOD WE MUST RECEIVE JESUS CHRIST.

Many people know *about* God, but don't know Him *personally*. The only way to know God personally is to receive Jesus Christ. So how can we receive Him?

Turn away from our sin. Jesus said, "The time has come. . . . Repent and believe the Good News!" (Mark 1:15) To repent means to *turn away* from sin.

Believe in Jesus. "Believe in the Lord Jesus, and you will be saved" (Acts 16:31). To believe means to *turn* to Jesus.

Respond to Jesus. Jesus promises, "Here I am! I stand at the door and knock. If anyone hears My voice and opens the door, I will go in and eat with him, and he with Me" (Revelation 3:20).

10

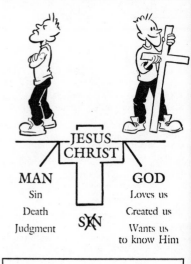

JESUS CHRIST

MAN	GOD
Sin	Loves us
Death	Created us
Judgment	Wants us to know Him

SIN

Where would you like to be?

11

Is there any good reason why you cannot receive Jesus Christ right now?

You can turn away from your sin and ask Jesus into your life now. You receive Jesus by praying to Him.

Prayer is simply talking to God. He will hear your prayer. Can you say this to God and mean it?

> *"Dear Lord Jesus,*
> *I know that You created me, love me, and want me to know You. My sin has kept me from knowing You. I turn from my sin. I receive Jesus Christ, who died to forgive my sin and rose from the dead to live in me. In Jesus' name, Amen."*

Now that you have received Jesus Christ, what happens?

12

JESUS CHANGES OUR LIVES WHEN WE KNOW HIM.

Receiving Jesus Christ is just the beginning. When He comes into our lives, we experience many changes—some immediately and others gradually.

A New Identity. "If anyone is in Christ, he is a new creation; the old has gone, the new has come!" (2 Corinthians 5:17)

Forgiveness. "As far as the east is from the west, so far has He removed our transgression (sin and guilt) from us" (Psalm 103:12).

Love. "We love because He first loved us" (1 John 4:19).

Freedom. "So if the Son sets you free, you will be free indeed" (John 8:36).

Confidence. "We have confidence before God because we obey His commands and do what pleases Him" (1 John 3:21-22).

Victory over Temptation. When you are tempted, He will also provide a way out so that you can stand up under it" (1 Corinthians 10:13).

Guidance. "Trust in the Lord with all your heart and lean not on your own understanding; in all your ways acknowledge Him, and He will make your paths straight" (Proverbs 3:5-6).

new identity · love · confidence · freedom · victory · forgiveness · guidance

How can we know Jesus even better?

FACT 6

WE MATURE AS WE KNOW JESUS BETTER.

You have now begun a relationship with Jesus. How can you grow in that relationship?

Spend time in prayer daily (Phil. 4:6).
_____ I will pray five minutes every day.

Study God's Word daily (2 Tim. 3:16).
_____ I will read one Bible chapter every day, beginning with the Book of Mark.

Submit to God consistently (James 1:22).
_____ I will obey God as I become aware of His instructions. I will get baptized as soon as possible (Acts 2:38).

Search for a church (Hebrews 10:24-25).
_____ I will go to a church that teaches clearly about Jesus.

15

Share Jesus with others (Romans 1:16).
_____ I will tell my family and best friend about my new relationship with Jesus Christ this week.

Seek Jesus completely (John 5:22-23).
_____ I will look to Jesus to change my attitudes and actions every day.

You probably feel you have a lot to learn. If you want further help in the decision you have made, write to:

Reach Out Ministries
3961 Holcomb Bridge Road 200
Norcross, GA 30092
(404) 441-2247

Barry

Scripture taken from the *Holy Bible, New International Version,* © 1973, 1978, 1984, International Bible Society. Used by permission of Zondervan Bible Publishers.

DYNAMIC DISCUSSION STARTERS FOR OUTREACH TO YOUR FRIENDS

You will be amazed at how open your friends will be to discuss the Gospel in a small group. (We call it Life Group. You may want to give it another name.) Through this discussion group you can provide an environment where you and your friends discuss the issues of God openly and naturally.

• **WHAT IS A LIFE GROUP?**
1. A place where friends can talk openly about what they believe without being put down by others.
2. A place where your friends can find love and acceptance.
3. A place where you can encourage your friends to take a serious look at Jesus Christ.

• **HOW DO YOU START A LIFE GROUP?**
1. The People—friends you are relating to and serving.
2. The Place—a familiar, comfortable place where you will not be interrupted: a classroom, a friend's home, the Burger King, etc.
3. The Time—a time you know most of your friends are free: after school, before school, Sunday night, etc. Plan to meet consistently for six weeks.
4. The Invitation—Target the friends you have been serving. Personally invite each one. The best size for discussion is five to ten people, but even if only one person responds, you will be successful. Let them know what you are doing and what to expect. You can say something like, "Several guys are going to get together each Friday morning at JJ's to have breakfast and talk about life, God, and our problems. Could you join us?"

• **HOW DO YOU LEAD A LIFE GROUP?**
You want to create a relaxed atmosphere so your friends can talk openly and freely. Look for opportunities to guide them toward Jesus, not shove Jesus down their throats.
Your role is to initiate discussion and then become a part

of the discussion as a friend. The foundation you have laid in prayer and serving will open doors for you to present the truth of Jesus Christ naturally.

Four powerful ingredients will help you lead a Life Group successfully.

1. Listen: Friends will share their most intimate concerns when you sincerely listen.

2. Accept: Respect others' points of view and their right to decide what to believe. Never put them down for what they believe. Try to understand and appreciate why they feel the way they do.

3. Encourage: Constantly affirm your friends' openness and willingness to work through what they believe.

4. Challenge: As you listen, accept, and encourage, you will be able to lovingly challenge your friends with the claims of Jesus Christ. The object is to present the Gospel and to challenge them to make a decision.

• WHAT CAN YOU DISCUSS IN A LIFE GROUP?

The following are sessions you can go through, each with an objective and questions you can use to start discussion. These are not set in concrete. It is up to you to discern where your friends are and the next step they need to take.

SESSION #1: A SAFE PLACE TO OPEN YOUR HEART

Objective: To build a foundation for communication.

Opening: Set the ground rules for communication.

1. Respect others' opinions. No laughing at or cutting another person down.

2. Speak one at a time. Give others the chance to express opinions.

3. Accept one another, even if the other person has a different opinion.

4. Honor each others' honesty. What is said in the group, stays in the group.

Question: "If God were to walk in this room right now, what two questions would you ask Him?"

Truth: "When Jesus reached the spot, He looked up and said, 'Zacchaeus come down immediately. I must stay at your house today.' So he came down at once and welcomed him gladly," (Luke 19: 5-6).

Preparation: Secure a place and time. Call your friends to remind them.

SESSION #2: IS THERE ANYTHING FOR SURE?

Objective: To create a thirst for a solution to life.

Questions:

- "Finish this sentence: Life is ...."
- "What event do you look forward to the most this year? (Such as Spring break, prom, etc.)" "Does it ever meet your expectations?"
- "What in your life can you always count on?"

Truth: "Everyone who drinks this water will be thirsty again, but whoever drinks the water I give him will never thirst. Indeed, the water I give him will become in him a spring of water welling up to eternal life," (John 4:13-14).

Preparation: Think through, then write out how Christ has been the "For Sure" in your life when other things have fallen through. Recall specific things in the world that have let you down, such as achievements, material possessions, etc. Tell how Christ was there to give you true fulfillment when these things didn't.

SESSION #3: SOMEONE WHO CARES.

Objective: To understand that God loves us.

Questions:

- "Finish this sentence: Love is...."
- "In your life, who really loves you?"
- "How do you know when someone loves you?"
- "Do you have any relationships that will always be there, even for eternity?"

Truth: "Never will I leave you, never will I forsake you," (Hebrews 13:5).

Preparation: Think through and write down specific times when you have felt lonely and no one cared about you. How did Christ help you through those times? Communicate how Christ stuck by you when others turned their backs.

SESSION #4: WHO'S TO BLAME FOR THIS MESS?

Objective: To explain the separation caused by man's sin.

Questions:
- "What do you think is the worst thing that has happened in our nation in the last year?"
- "If God is a God of love, why do you think bad things happen?"

Truth: "For all have sinned and fall short of the glory of God," (Romans 3:23). "For the wages of sin is death but the gift of God is eternal life in Christ Jesus our Lord," (Romans 6:23).

Preparation: Write out examples of how God has provided us with all of the resources to feed all people, but because of man's sin and selfishness, people are homeless and starving.

SESSION #5: THE ULTIMATE GIFT.

Objective: To show how God paid for our sin through the death and resurrection of Jesus Christ.

Questions:
- "What is the worst thing anyone has ever done to you?"
- "How did that affect your relationship?"
- "What would it take for you to restore that relationship?"

Truth: "For God so loved the world that He gave His one and only Son, that whoever believes in Him shall not perish but have eternal life," (John 3:16).

Preparation: Write out and communicate the Gospel (*The Facts of Life* booklet will help you with that).

SESSION #6: OPENING THE DOOR.

Objective: To challenge y our friends to decide to follow Christ.

Questions:
- "Have you ever felt close to God?" "When?"
- "What do you think keeps you close to God all the time?"
- "Do you think it is possible to be close to God all the time?"

Truth: "Here I am! I stand at the door and knock. If anyone hears my voice and opens the door, I will come in and eat with him, and he with me," (Revelations 3:20).

Preparation: Write out and communicate your personal testimony emphasizing how you made the decision to follow Jesus.

Ask the others in the group if they are interested in knowing God personally like you do.

FOLLOW UP

After you have completed the sessions as a group, decide the next step. You might want to ask them if they want to continue meeting. Or follow up your conversations with them one on one. If they accept Christ, follow through with the booklet, *Getting Started.* This can be a good focus for the group if it continues, and if several of your friends accept Christ.

HOW TO LEAD A GROUP THROUGH TAKING YOUR CAMPUS FOR CHRIST

The point of TAKING YOUR CAMPUS FOR CHRIST is to put what you are learning into *action*. The best way to do that is take a group through the book putting it into *action together*.

The purpose of this Leader's Guide is to help you do that in a way that will maximize your personal influence on the campus, as well as creating a campus movement in which students are coming to Christ.

My hope is that Romans 1:16 will become a reality for everyone who reads this book: "I am not ashamed of the Gospel, because it is the power of God for the salvation of everyone who believes."

YOU AS THE LEADER
You may be asking: "Who should lead the group on our campus or at our church?" You! Actually there are two types of leaders for a group going through this book.

1. *Students* who have a desire to see God create a powerful spiritual movement on your campus. You may not feel adequate, trained, old enough, or mature enough. But you do know that God has given you a desire to see your campus know Christ. Go ahead. Take the risk. God will honor you stepping out in faith.
2. *Youth leaders* who have a burden to see the campus (es) they are responsible for reached with the message of Jesus Christ. You can take all or part of your youth group through this book. Remember that you only

want the students going through it who really want to make a difference on their campus.

Being the leader will require more time and personal involvement than the others who are going through the book will give. So before you decide to lead, sit down and count the cost.

To get prepared to lead, here are some of the things you will need to do.

1. *Read through the book.* Make sure that you work through the material in the book before you take the group through it. Ask God to show you how to lead the group.
2. *Organize the group.* Get a few other students who you know are interested in this and discuss the idea with them. Then announce it to the larger group—your campus Christian group or your youth group. At an introductory meeting explain what is involved in the meetings, the assignments, the time and place of the meetings. Explain that it will be action-oriented with each one expected to read the material, and then to put the material into practice. One creative idea is to have all of these people over to your house or at a restaurant for pizza so you can get started in a fun, relaxed way.
3. *Purchase the materials.* Well in advance of the first meeting, order a book for every person in the group. To get the most out of the group it will be good for each person to have THE TIME ALONE NOTEBOOK, and THE FACTS OF LIFE also. See the back of the book for the instructions on ordering the material. Make sure everyone brings their Bible.
4. *Decide the best time and place to meet.* Decide on a morning before school when the meeting will fit the most people's schedule. Or you can meet after school or at night. You will need *one hour* to go through each week's session. If you need more time to discuss the issues addressed that week, then take an extra week to talk about them. *Don't rush through the sessions.* The

best place to meet will be either at a room on your campus, or at a restaurant or home close to your school.

5. *Inform your pastor or youth leaders.* This will be easy if you are doing this in your youth group. But even if you are doing it at school you need to keep church leaders informed.

THE BEST MEETINGS

In order for each week to be an exciting, dynamic time together, you need to keep several important points in mind.

1. *Be prepared.* Begin your preparation for each session at least five days in advance. This has two aspects:
   - Preparing the material in the book. It is more than reading and doing Bible study. You need to put the material into practice yourself.
   - Preparing for the session. You need to go through the suggested schedule for each session and decide what you will do for that session.

2. *Start on time.* Do this each week even if everyone is not there at the starting time. That keeps the people who are on time from feeling like you are wasting their time.

3. *Form into groups of three.* Do this at the first session so that people will be accountable to two other people for taking action on the book. One important key is for everyone to come prepared. Nothing will cause you to lose momentum like a lackadaisical attitude. If someone is not preparing speak to him about it. If it continues ask him to consider dropping out of the group. The groups of three will help each person be prepared and take action.

4. *Make the group sessions dynamic.* This will happen when your focus is on the Lord, and on reaching your friends. You will want to encourage discussion, but primarily you want them to report on what the Lord is showing them and what they are putting into action. Here are some hints on how to do that.

   - State clearly what you want them to discuss or to do.
   - Respect each person's comments.

- Stay close to the Scriptures.
- Challenge trite and superficial answers.
- Involve everyone in the discussion, not just the vocal ones.
- Evaluate after each session to see how you can improve.

5. *Pray a lot.* Pray for the group as a whole as well as for the individuals in it. Ask the Lord to make this group a mighty force for His kingdom on your campus. Ask Him to build a spiritual momentum that will bring many people on your campus to Jesus Christ.

TAKING YOUR CAMPUS FOR CHRIST ACTION GROUP

MEETING #1—TOTALLY OUT OF SIGHT

- Welcome everyone. [2 minutes]
- Do an icebreaker like: Speak to three different people, telling each one a different reason why you like school cafeteria food. [5 minutes]
- Break into groups of 3. Discuss personal needs and pray for each other. [10 minutes]
- What would it take for God to do on your campus what He did on Jacob's campus? [5 minutes]
- Outline on the board specific ways that God could use this group that would be beyond your imagination. [10 minutes.]
- Read John 1:35-42 out loud. Ask the question: "What do you want?" (No response needed.)
- In groups of 3 ask each person to share specifically what decisions they have made about

Choices

    —choices they have made about their money, time, and possessions,

    —choices about baggage from what other people have done to them.

    —choices they have made about old actions and attitudes

Time

    —how they will give Jesus their undivided attention

Friends and school
—how they will bring their friends to Jesus
Have each person design one action point from all this to share with the group. [15 minutes]
- Bringing the whole group together, ask each one to tell his one action point to the whole group. [15 minutes]
- Give them the assignment to do chapter 2 for next week.

MEETING #2—COMPLETELY LACKING

- Focus on the purpose and goals of the meeting. Write the purpose on the board or on a poster: TO PUT INTO ACTION ROMANS 1:16. Talk about what that means. Get into small groups to discuss it, then each group give a report to the larger group. [15 minutes]
- Using the quotes by Eddie Murphy and Pascal talk about why people at your school are not interested in hearing about God's love for them. Use the small group to discuss and the large group to report. [10 minutes]
- Read Jimmie's poem on page 30-31. In their small group ask them to describe one person they know who is hurting. [5 minutes]
- Ask them what they think it will take to bring that person to Jesus Christ. [5 minutes]
- Many people have empty, broken hearts at school. Ask them how they want God to use them to reach friends who are hurting with the message of Jesus Christ. Have 4–5 share that with the whole group. [10 minutes]
- In the small groups pray for hurting friends, and for a burden to reach them for Jesus Christ. [5 minutes]
- Give the assignment to complete chapter 3 for next week.

MEETING #3—AWESOMELY EXPERIENCING GOD
- Read the quote from Madalyn Murray O'Hair. Then say, "Today we want to have an honest discussion about the reality of Jesus in our lives." [1 minute]

- Have someone read Matthew 14:25-31. [2 minutes]
- In groups of three name one area of your life where you are in your "comfort zone" but you know you need to "get out of the boat" [5 minutes]
- Pray in the groups of three. Put one person in the middle of the group, then the other two pray for him about the area he mentioned. Then do the same with the other two. [10 minutes]
- Now invite them to experience God right now. Tell them that the rest of the meeting is a time to get out of the boat and walk to Jesus. Ask them to be quiet and let God speak to them about what they need to do, then go do it. If someone needs to call parents and ask forgiveness, do it. If someone needs to accept Christ, do it. If someone needs to go to another person in the room to get a relationship right, you have permission. Listen to God, encounter Him, then do whatever He tells you to step out of the boat. [45 minutes]
- Remind them to do chapter 4 for next week.

MEETING #4—DEFINITELY CHANGING AND REARRANGING
NOTE: This could be a very serious time. Allow it to be that way. *If the spirit of God is moving, don't quench it by going on to something else. But don't let it drag either.*

- Begin by asking them to share what they did in the last week to step out of the boat and experience God. [10 minutes]
- If people turned in a report about everything they had seen you do, what would they write? Be honest. Share this in groups of three. [5–10 minutes]
- Focus on the "7 Questions" on page 117. Ask them to go through the "7 Questions" writing down specific sins that they need to confess to God. [10–15 minutes]
- With the whole group go through each question and allow people to confess those sins. (James 5:16) Be sensitive. Ask them to be specific. You begin. [15–20 minutes]
- Read 1 John 1:9. Remind them that Jesus has taken away all of their sin. Then read Ephesians 5:18. Lead them in a prayer to release the Holy Spirit in them.

"Lord, right now I release Your Spirit in my life. Fill me with Your Life. I receive the gift of Your Spirit right now. In Jesus name." [5 minutes]
- Before you leave practice breathing. Remind them to do that spiritually this week. [3 minutes]
- Tell them to come prepared with chapter 5.

MEETING # 5—PASSIONATELY ROMANTIC

NOTE: Prepare a Bible Response Sheet and a Prayer Action Sheet for each person from the back of this book. Take a group order for the *TIME ALONE WITH GOD NOTE-BOOK* if they have not ordered it already.
- Have them share in small groups one significant answer to prayer in their own lives. [5 minutes]
- Read the S.D. Gordon quote on page 63. On a scale of 1–10 how would you rate the time you spend with God? Write a number down. Where do you want it to be? What do you need to do to get it there? Discuss that in groups of three. [5 minutes]
- Have each person fill out the Bible Response Sheet. Ask them to listen carefully to what God is saying to them out of that passage. Focus on John 14:12-14. [10 minutes]
- Have each person fill out the Prayer Action Sheet. Use it as a time to talk to God. [5–7 minutes]
- In groups of three share their application from the passage and their one major prayer request. Pray for each other.
- With the whole group allow them to ask questions about spending time alone with God. Don't feel like you have to know all of the answers. Let everyone talk.
- Challenge them to the "15:30 Experiment"—to spend 15 minutes a day alone with God for the next 30 days. Ask them to make that commitment by telling one other person that that is what they will do.
- Remind them that it is in this time that the Lord will prepare them to be a powerful influence on the campus.
- Tell them to be prepared with chapter 6 for next week.

MEETING #6—ULTIMATELY THE POWER WEAPON

NOTE: Write on the board—"In Jesus I'm Satan's Personal Nightmare."

- Read 1 Peter 5:8. How do you see Satan "roaring" at our school? Make a list on the board. [5 minutes]
- Read 1 Peter 5:10. According to that verse what does God want to do in and through us? [5 minutes]
- One very specific way you can be Satan's Personal Nightmare is to become a part of a PRAYER POWER TEAM. Get with the two people whose names you wrote down in your book on page 83. (Work with the confusion until everyone gets settled with two other people.) [5–10 minutes]
- Have them discuss the three times during the week that they will pray. Have them write those down. [5 minutes]
- Now have them write down the names of their non-Christian friends they will pray for. [5 minutes]
- Spend the rest of the time in their PRAYER POWER TEAMS praying for each other and for each of their non-Christian friends. [30 minutes]
- Remind them to do chapter 7 for next week. Come prepared.

MEETING #7—INTENSELY LOVING

- Begin the meeting in the PRAYER POWER TEAMS. Tell them this can be one of the times they meet this week. Give them plenty of time to pray for each other and for their three non-believing friends. [10–15 minutes]
- Do the survey with the entire group that they did on page 88. Ask how many of them came to Christ because a specific person cared for them. Ask several to tell who that was and how that happened. [10 minutes]
- In their PRAYER POWER TEAMS have them tell the "unlovable" person whose name they wrote down and the two creative ways they will serve that person this week. Have them pray for each other and for the people they will serve. Pray for God's love to shine

through. [10 minutes]
- Make a list on the board of several creative ways the group can be Jesus "with skin on." Decide which *one* of those you will put into practice this week. [10 minutes]
- Pray with the whole group that the Lord will use you to serve your friends and your school. [10 minutes]

MEETING #8—NATURALLY COMMUNICATING
- Meet in PRAYER POWER TEAMS. After praying for your three unbelieving friends, decide which one you want to talk to about Christ first. Have a focused prayer time for that person. [15 minutes]
- Talk about how you would like to approach that person, and how you will get into the conversation. Remember to focus on their needs. What need does your friend have that you can talk about? (See page 102 to review the questions.) [5 minutes]
- Each person share his personal testimony in the groups of three. If time allows give it two or three times for the practice. Encourage them to help each other by pointing out strengths and places where they might improve. [10–15 minutes]
- Using *THE FACTS OF LIFE* booklet, divide into twos and practice going over it with each other. Use the transition questions to get into the booklet. Especially focus on what you will do on Fact #4. [15 minutes]
- If the group wants to you can continue to meet to pray and talk about how you will love, serve, and share with your friends and you school. Discuss this. [15 minutes]

CONTINUING TO MEET
- Meet again next week to report on the conversations you had during the week.
- Dicuss how you will follow up those who respond using the *GETTING STARTED* booklet.
- Talk about how you can widen your circle of influence by praying for more unbelievers, loving and serving more, and sharing Christ more.
- Ask each person if he will accept the challenge of sharing Christ with at least one person every week.

- Continue to meet to pray, encourage each other in your witnessing, and discovering how you can make Romans 1:16 a reality in your school.

For students and youth workers—Here are resources to help you move ahead! You can find them at your local Christian bookstore. Or for more information write to: Reach Out Ministries, 3961 Holcomb Bridge Road, Suite 201, Norcross, GA 30092.

The *Moving Toward Maturity Series* by Barry St. Clair

Each of these books builds on the one before to help you grow in your relationship with Jesus Christ.

Following Jesus (Book 1) What does it really mean to be a disciple of Jesus Christ? This book lets you find out for yourself.
ISBN: 0-89693-290-7   Catalog no. 6-1290

Spending Time Alone with God (Book 2) Learn how to set up and follow through on a regular daily time with God.
ISBN: 0-89693-292-3   Catalog no. 6-1292

Making Jesus Lord (Book 3) Discover how to give Jesus top priority in your life—and how that makes everyday living an adventure.
ISBN: 0-89693-293-1   Catalog no. 6-1293

Giving Away Your Faith (Book 4) Learn the best ways to share your relationship with Jesus Christ with your friends.
ISBN: 0-89693-297-4   Catalog no. 6-1297

Influencing Your World (Book 5) Helps you explore practical ways to serve unselfishly and reach out to your world.
ISBN: 0-89693-294-X   Catalog no. 6-1294

The Facts of Life—A sixteen-page booklet that clearly explains the basics of the Gospel
ISBN: 1-56476-141-X   Catalog no. 6-3141

Getting Started—A 32-page booklet that provides a step-by-step discipleship program for the newest believers.
ISBN: 1-56476-142-8   Catalog no. 6-3142

Time Alone with God Notebook—Contains all you need to begin a daily quiet time with God. Provides instructions and sheets to guide your time.
ISBN 1-56476-143-6   Catalog no. 6-3143

Penetrating the Campus—A great book for youth workers who want to reach out to students where they are. By Barry St. Clair and Keith Naylor.
ISBN: 1-56476-085-5   Catalog no. 6-3085

Moving Toward Maturity Leader's Book—Leader's guides for the entire Moving Toward Maturity Series. It also includes reproducible sheets for group Bible study.
ISBN: 0-89693-298-2   Catalog no. 6-1298

Building Leaders for Strategic Youth Ministry—This training guide helps adults work with young people and lead them to maturity in Christ. Learn to pinpoint student needs, train, and encourage student disciples.
ISBN: 0-89693-288-5   Catalog no. 6-1288

Reach Out Strategy (Video)—A six-part, 2 1/2-hour video seminar by Barry St. Clair for youth workers.
Catalog number 8-7640.